ON THE
MEANING
OF THE
UNIVERSITY

Eric Ashby
Brand Blanshard
John W. Gardner
T. R. McConnell
Mina Rees
David Pierpont Gardner

ON THE
MEANING
OF THE
UNIVERSITY

Edited and with an Introductory Essay by

Sterling M. McMurrin

University of Utah Press

378.73
O58

Copyright © 1976 by The University of Utah Press,
Salt Lake City, Utah 84112. All rights reserved.
Library of Congress Catalog Card No. 74-22637.
International Standard Book No. 0-87480-097-8.
David P. Gardner's essay is drawn from his contribution
to Volume VII of a major project of the Commission on Critical Choices
for Americans, to be published in fourteen volumes
in 1976 by Lexington Books, D. C. Heath & Company,
and appears by permission of the publisher.
© 1976 by The Third Century Corporation.
All rights reserved.

Essays upon the occasion
of the inauguration of David Pierpont Gardner
as tenth president of the University of Utah,
November 19, 1973.

40666

North Carolina Wesleyan College Library
Rocky Mount, North Carolina 27801

Preface

The essays of this volume were written to celebrate the inauguration of David Pierpont Gardner as the tenth president of the University of Utah. President Gardner's paper was prepared for the Commission on Critical Choices for Americans. The essays are addressed to the general subject "The Meaning of the University in the Late Twentieth Century."

Lord Ashby, Master of Clare College of Cambridge University, is one of the most widely celebrated educators in the English-speaking world. His leadership in education extends far beyond the United Kingdom to every continent. Professor Brand Blanshard of Yale University, one of the foremost living philosophers, is known throughout the world as a leading rationalist and idealist. A forthcoming volume in the Library of Living Philosophers, *The Philosophy of Brand Blanshard*, will be an extensive critical examination of his philosophical ideas. Dr. John W. Gardner, former president of the Carnegie Corporation and of the Carnegie Foundation for the Advancement of Teaching, and former Secretary of Health, Education and Welfare, is the founder and chairman of Common Cause. In intellectual circles his name is virtually synonymous with the terms "excellence" and "self-renewal." Professor T. R. McConnell, who writes and speaks with a voice of uncommon authority, is the dean of American scholars in the field of higher education. He is perhaps best known as past chairman of the Center for Research and Development in Higher Education at the University of California, Berkeley. A distinguished mathematician and teacher of mathematics, Dr. Mina Rees of the City University of New York has had a large impact on American scholarship as an administrator of scientific research and of advanced education. A past director of the Mathematical Sciences Division of the Office of Naval Research, she became the first president of the Graduate School and University Center of the City University after its reorganization in 1972. Dr. David Pierpont Gardner, formerly vice president of the University of California, is an expert in the recent developments in higher education that relate especially to the new methods and forms of teaching and the extension of learning both on and beyond the campus. His exceptional scholarly talents are exhibited in his volume *The California Oath Controversy*, the standard work on the subject. Rarely has a group of writers of such extensive talents been brought together in a volume of original essays on education.

The authors wish to express their appreciation to Norma B. Mikkelsen, director of the University of Utah Press, and to Trudy McMurrin, who was Press editor for this volume.

S. M. M.

The University of Utah

Contents

Sterling M. McMurrin

The Philosophy of Education

For wisdom in the philosophy of education we should turn to many sources — to the philosophers, scientists, scholars, artists, executives, educators, students, and laymen who have something important to say about the meaning, purpose, and value of education. Often there is more to be learned from the experience and judgments of these than from typical professional statements in educational philosophy. For such statements all too commonly exhibit the artificiality of preconceived systems and employ formally structured categories and conventional textbook arguments.

Education is an intricately complex set of living institutions. The formally devised descriptions and prescriptions that are developed and disseminated in the schools themselves often fail to grasp the real vitality, complexity, and diversity of the educational process and fail therefore to express the full meaning and value of education. This is a volume on the philosophy of education which avoids formality and artificiality by drawing from the thought and living experience of persons of high competence in educational matters, whose impressions, attitudes, and ideas have been generated and affected by a variety of conditions and interests and within diverse contexts of philosophical views and practical commitments.

Whatever else it may be, education quite certainly is basically a function of the culture. It serves the life instincts of the culture, for at its roots it is a society's instinctive effort to strengthen, preserve, and extend itself, to secure its own future through the criticism and perpetuation of established conventions, institutions, ideals, and practices. Its character is determined largely by the character of the culture; variations and changes in the culture yield changes in the substance and processes of education. This does not mean that education is simply a reflection of other elements of the culture, for education is the most powerful instrument for effecting change in the total culture and in its social institutions.

This is of basic importance for the philosophy of education, as the philosophy of education is essentially the discipline of defining the meaning of education, determining its purposes, and establishing its substantive foundations. It is unfortunate that those who pursue the philosophy of education professionally have often sought the ground of educational policy and practice not in the facts of their own culture, or the cultures of the world, but rather in speculative metaphysics or epistemology, or at best in the theory of value. It is obvious that educational philosophy cannot be indifferent to metaphysics, epistemology, or value theory — especially value theory; in various ways these impinge upon the principles and policies of education and they are therefore not irrelevant. A conception of human nature, for instance, or basic moral ideas that have broad acceptance in a culture should not be ignored by educators. But this is not primarily because philosophical theories on the nature of reality or the structure of knowledge or the meaning of the good are essential foundations for the philosophy of education. Rather it is because such theories may themselves be important elements of the culture with both theoretical and practical implications and are therefore inevitably related to education. Educational policy and practice cannot be logically deduced, as some have supposed, from the specific theories which commonly describe the several major types of philosophy, such as idealism, realism, pragmatism, or existentialism. Education is a practical art and it is an exercise in futility to attempt to design educational theories, policies, and practices that logically follow from the basic propositions which define those philosophies.

The essays that comprise this volume are concerned with a variety of facets of education and the conditions that affect it, and they therefore make various contributions to the philosophy of education. Their vitality and timeliness issue from the fact that while each is distinctive in conception, form, and content, it draws both its substance and its arguments from a consideration of actual cultural and social facts and ideas. Whatever their commitments or inclinations, the authors here are not attempting to prescribe for education by imposing formulae which have been deduced from the findings of speculative philosophy. Their statements exhibit a sensitivity to the fundamental character and quality of our culture and a knowledge of the difficult problems which confront our social institutions, but they are equally engaged with those mundane matters which inevitably claim the time and energies of educators and especially of those who seek education.

If the philosophy of education were deducible from metaphysical systems, it presumably would be in principle possible to arrive at the "true" philosophy of education, and thereby to identify "absolute" purposes of education. For metaphysical claims are truth claims and, if indeed meaningful, their implicates are likewise true or false. There would be a true or false philosophy of education as there might be a true or false theology or physics. But if the philosophy of education is itself — like education — a function of the culture, as I believe it properly is, it is not appropriate to argue that an educational philosophy is true or false or that one philosophy is nearer the truth than another, although, of course, it may be more logical or more attuned to the facts. The question is, rather, one of a philosophy's appropriateness to the culture in which it is developed. An educational principle or policy must be judged somewhat pragmatically in terms of its relevance to the defining character of the culture. There can be no claim to educational absolutes. Fundamental changes in the culture, which are inevitable, entail correlative changes in the principles of education.

On this interpretation, of course, philosophies of education can appropriately compete for acceptance within a society or culture. Since it would necessarily place primary emphasis on the individual, an educational philosophy that is fitting for the United States would obviously have much to recommend it to Canada, France, or Great Britain, though perhaps not to Russia, China, or Albania. And an educational philosophy fashioned for Hitler's Germany would hardly be acceptable to today's educators in West Germany.

This is simply to argue that a philosophy of education should be generated out of the concrete experience of a society, where that experience covers the entire spectrum from the moral, aesthetic, and spiritual ideals of creative thinkers to the grossest facts of human struggle and failure as these are seen in the political and economic travail of a people. Educational policies are not necessarily unrelated to some abstractions of metaphysics, and certainly they have much to do with specific theories of value, but if they are to have a constructive impact on the lives of individuals and the life of a society they must be authentic responses to the concrete conditions of that society and its culture. Those conditions indeed include the philosophical systems and moral and aesthetic ideals of a people, but they include also the social, political, economic, biological, psychological, and technological facts that set the limits and provide the elemental materials of human existence. Whether the dominant philosophy of a culture is idealistic or realistic is an important matter. But it is less important to educational policy and practice than whether the people are plagued by poverty or enjoy comparative affluence, whether they live under tyranny or enjoy the political amenities of democracy, whether they are engrossed in chronic warfare or have the benefits of a stable peace.

If a society and its culture are to avoid comparative stagnation or actual decline, the educative process must be critical and creative as well as conservative, and its critical and creative activities must be supported at the least by a strong and effective minority. That support is essential to its meaning and purpose. Certainly in a culture that is committed ideally to the primary worth of the individual person and that is characterized by scientific intelligence and technological achievement, the critical and creative capacities of education must be not merely tolerated but rather aggressively cultivated and strengthened. Anything less would not only betray the ideals of the culture but would as well contribute to the eventual disintegration of the social institutions. It is a paradox that the very preservation of a complex society requires its change. Moreover, it is when education becomes critical and creative that it releases the individual from total bondage to society and effectively contributes to the cultivation of authentic individuality in the person and individualism in the social order. If it is the error of some to fail to recognize that the conserving function is proper to educational institutions, it is the great error of most majorities to suppose that the perpetuation of established ideas, modes, and techniques is the only appropriate end of education.

It is possible to say that when they are conceived broadly in terms of the large movements and issues that claim the energies of a people, and when their relation to the value structure of both the individual and society is recognized, the purposes of education are at least three-fold: to bring strength and vitality and lasting power to the culture; to conserve, criticize, improve, and perpetuate the social institutions; and to contribute to the achievement of authentic individuality and the well-being of the individual. I refer, of course, to education in a democratic society, one which has a tradition of individualism and is committed to the achievement of the ideals of freedom. Here, as I believe the essays of this volume clearly indicate, it is an assumed principle that whatever contributes to the integrity and quality of life of the individual person will improve the institutions of society and bring greater strength to the culture. At least this is the faith of those committed to the ideals of freedom and for their society it is the large task of education to ensure that this faith is justified.

Beyond the definition of the basic meanings and purposes of education, the philosophy of education must be concerned with several areas of concrete issues and problems that confront the actual pursuit and practice of education. Among these are the goals of the various types of educational institutions, the objectives of instruction, the substance of education, the methods of instruction, perhaps even the management and finance of education, and the education of educators. A few comments on these matters may be appropriate.

In its entirety, of course, education is a responsibility of the total society. The schools, colleges, and universities perform a quite specialized function. To define that function, it seems to me, to set limits for the formal institutionalized pursuit of education, is one of the basic tasks of the philosophy of education. I find it quite impossible to describe the basic task of schools, colleges, and universities on any other ground than as an intellectual enterprise: that of knowledge and reason — the achievement and dissemination of knowledge, the investigation of its practical applications, and discipline in the right uses of reason. Our society places innumerable other tasks upon the schools. Some of these are entirely appropriate, but many of them are not properly the responsibility of schools and should be resisted by them. They should be performed by other social agencies; they have been imposed upon the schools only because of society's failures elsewhere.

I do not mean to circumscribe the meanings of knowledge and reason in a narrowly restrictive way. Certainly, for example, it is the task of a school or university to contribute to the moral education of the individual and the moral strength of society. In describing education as an intellectual enterprise I mean to include not only basic knowledge, but its fundamental applications in technology as well, and not only science, but also the liberal and fine arts. And by intellectual I mean not only the pursuit of knowledge and reason as ends in themselves, or as instruments in achieving other ends, but also the cultivation of the moral, artistic, and spiritual life. Education conceived on this broad basis will not only enhance the quality of life of the individual but will bring strength to the culture and the social institutions. My point here is the simple one of holding, for instance, that while moral education is an appropriate and necessary task of the schools and colleges, their specific responsibility to moral education lies in providing the knowledge and rational discrimination relevant to value judgment and moral decision. To provide an intellectual component to the moral life is consonant with their basic purpose and is, moreover, essential to effective moral development. They are not responsible for moral education in its entirety, for this is a matter which must inevitably engage a wide spectrum of social and cultural forces and influences and which reaches far beyond the capability of the schools. The same principle holds in matters pertaining to the relation of formal schooling to the artistic and spiritual facets of experience.

That knowledge and reason are basic to the primary meaning and large purposes of education for our culture means, of course, that the basic objective of instruction is essentially cognitive. It is concerned first with literacy, the linguistic and mathematical facility for obtaining and communicating knowledge, and with the techniques of rational implication. It involves such diverse matters as the discernment of fact, some sense of the interrelationship of facts, the analysis of meanings, recognition of causal relationships, a grasp of the principles of explanation, theory construction, and the distinction of universals and particulars. The strong Hellenic element in the origins and development of our culture probably accounts for its pronounced cognitive bias and its preoccupation with reason and knowledge, a trend that has eventuated in advanced theoretical science and the technology which science has engendered as well as a general intellectual climate of what might be called scientific intelligence.

But cognitive matters, though basic to our intellectual life and of inestimable importance, are not the whole character of our culture; they are by no means the only facet of our make-up and experience large enough to make a legitimate claim upon formal education. Our cultural tradition is romantic and affective as well as rational and cognitive; we are beings of sentiment, emotion, and passion, as well as of thought and knowledge. More than that, the practical necessities of personal life, the functional needs of our social institutions, and the increasing demand for intelligent and informed decision-making by everyone are constant reminders that education is inevitably engrossed in the volitional or conative element of the individual's experience and the corresponding action orientation of the social order. Education must be concerned not only with the cognitive and affective, but also with the cultivation and discipline of the capacities and habits of will, decision, and action.

Far from being independent of one another, the several objectives of instruction, *cognitive*, *affective*, and *conative*, are intimately and imperceptibly intermingled and involved, and one of the basic challenges of both educational policy and the instructional or learning process is the achievement of an effective relationship among them. When this is not accomplished, education fails to realize the important practical end of the individual and social capacity for a life tempered by knowledge and reason, and for intelligent value discrimination and rational action.

Since the philosophy of education is concerned primarily with the purposes or ends of education, it is necessarily involved with the substance of education — the curriculum and its content. Here there are at least two matters deserving comment that are basic to contemporary educational policy in our society: the meaning and nature of "liberal education," and the question of whether the full spectrum of experience is represented in the curriculum of the schools and colleges.

"Liberal education" seems to have originally referred to that education appropriate for the liberal or free man. Those who were not free were expected to follow more practical pursuits. I believe that it is this meaning that has led to our present habit of distinguishing between liberal and vocational, or what is now more commonly called "technical," education, a distinction that has unfortunately divided the educational establishment against itself and even now continues to rob a large portion of our population of adequate liberal instruction in the sciences, humanities, and fine arts. Today's meaning of a liberal education, I believe, should be an education that "liberalizes," or frees, a person — frees him from the bondage of ignorance, incompetence, bigotry, superstition, habit, and irrationality. It is the education that contributes most directly to the achievement of the ideal of free persons in a free society and is in principle, therefore, an education on which every person in our society has a just claim.

Moreover, liberal education as now conceived is not useless and impractical, as many still insist. On the contrary, it is eminently practical, as it is essential to the pursuit not only of numerous vocations but of the full, satisfying life as well. In my opinion, the common distinction and separation of liberal from vocational or technical education should be overcome, not only in our philosophy but also in our institutional policies and practices. To provide education that both satisfies occupational interests and needs and cultivates a genuine liberality in the individual is one of the most critical challenges currently confronting our educational establishment. It will not be adequately met until a major change is effected in our educational thought. This does not at all mean that all persons should follow the same curriculum in their education or that all institutions should become alike in their purposes and pursuits. The destruction of diversity among schools and colleges as among individuals would move us toward a deadening boredom and mediocrity of life. But it does mean that in a society committed to the freedom of the individual, every person should have access to opportunities that can provide him or her with an education that is useful and that genuinely contributes to authentic freedom.

The problem of education's relation to the full spectrum of experience is especially difficult. The various elements of individual and social experience add up to a vast and highly intricate complex of factors that are perhaps quite impossible to sort out for educational purposes: physical, biological, economic, intellectual, moral, artistic, and spiritual, to mention simply the most basic categories. But this means that since every person is involved in that total experiential complex, everyone should have at least some educational involvement in matters of science, technology, art, morals, and religion.

It is in science, of course, and in its implications for technology, that we have had the greatest success. But that is due to the fact that our culture with its intellectual set is eminently geared to cognitive pursuits and that our society, including the schools, provides more adequate rewards in this department than in others. We are improving in the fine arts but are woefully inadequate in our expenditure of resources and energy on education in the arts. In matters of morals and religion we are rather dismal failures. By morals in education I mean, as I have already indicated, the pursuit of knowledge and rationality relevant to moral discrimination, not engagement in moral dogma or propaganda. And by religion in education, of course, I mean not the dissemination of dogma but the contribution of knowledge and rationality to the achievement of a spiritual quality of life, the investiture of life with meaning, purpose, and commitment. Here are areas of basic experience that have been seriously short-changed by our educational philosophies, policies, and instructional practices.

The central philosophical issue found in the large area of problems in the methods of education, which ranges all the way from the merits or evils of the lecture system to the employment of computers in instruction, is the relationship of means to ends. It was the great merit of John Dewey as a moral philosopher to insist that ends should not be considered independently of the means for their realization, nor means independently of their practical relevance to ends. Inevitably means have some determining effect on the character of ends, and institutional means or the means of instruction can make a difference in the fulfillment or failure of the purposes, goals, and objectives of education. A basic task of educators is to ensure that, whatever their impact, the means of instruction do not become the chief determinants of the ends, that ends are established within the realistic context of available and effective methods but are determined ultimately by value considerations that are genuinely humane.

The difficult problems relating to the management and financing of today's educational institutions and processes are not immune to philosophic consideration. They generally fall within the scope of moral, political, and economic philosophy, but they are issues in the philosophy of education nevertheless. I have in mind such matters as the definition of intellectual freedom and the establishment of its necessary and sufficient conditions; the determination of specific institutional goals; decisions affecting the student clientele, such as admissions and retention; the issue of the politicization of a university campus; or even the question of whether some types of public and private money, e.g., federal funds or income from certain kinds of investment, will be employed for specified educational purposes. The concreteness and specificity of problems of management, or what some may prefer to call governance or administration, should not obscure the underlying and often difficult philosophical issues that must be faced if these problems are to be treated effectively.

In conclusion, I call attention to a matter of major importance in the education of educators, both administrators and teachers. I refer to the need for more adequate attention to both the philosophy of education and the science of education. Education as a profession is an art, a fine and practical art, and like all arts it requires the vision of philosophy, which determines its meaning and its purposes, and the discipline of the sciences, which provides the factual and theoretical bases for its practical pursuits. I have already argued for reform of the current professional philosophy of education. What is needed on the other side, at least in most institutions, is greater breadth in the conception of the science of education. Too commonly it is assumed that psychological studies satisfy the scientific demands on an education in education. Certainly even more work is needed here, particularly in the psychology of the learning process on its noncognitive side. But desperately needed also is a more adequate treatment of the sociological and anthropological, and even biological and physical, foundations of the many problems that learners and teachers must inevitably encounter. Until this greater breadth in the relevant sciences is provided in the preparation of educators their education will be seriously deficient.

The essays of this volume do not cover all facets of the philosophy of education. They were not intended to be general or systematic statements, nor were they planned as a group to provide a systematic coverage of the problems. Rather, they are responses to an invitation simply to comment on the meaning of a university in our time. But together they are a major contribution to the philosophy of education, for they have issued from extensive experience in the practical problems of learning and of educational institutions, and from authentic wisdom in judgment on matters pertaining to the character of our culture and social institutions and the purposes and substance of education.

Eric Ashby

Reconciliation of Tradition and Modernity in Universities

The installation of a university president highlights a perpetual challenge to universities: how to reconcile tradition with innovation. On one hand the new president hopes to improve the institution, and his colleagues (without impugning the regime of his predecessor) hope he will bring new ideas into the administration. On the other hand his freedom of manœuvre is constrained, because the institution is the embodiment of an ancient tradition whose roots lie far deeper than the date when the university was founded; they lie in the academic legacy inherited from the universities of Europe. The college where I am sitting as I write this essay has been on this site since 1326. The concept of what a university stands for, whether the university is in Utah or Cambridge, rests on seven centuries of institutional evolution. Over these centuries there have been changes and reforms, and the fittest of these have survived to constitute the concept of what we now mean by a university. Innovations which might erode this concept would cut the university off from its roots; but lack of innovation, failure to adapt the institution to the social climate, would lead to extinction. So, in a sense, innovation in universities is like innovation in the breeding of crops. A lot can be done and needs to be done, but it has to be done within the hereditary constraints of the species. Innovations which defy these constraints are dangerous and unlikely to be viable.

So the installation of a president is an occasion to reflect on the resolution of forces between tradition and modernity, not specifically for the university of Utah (that would be impertinent from an invited guest to this volume) but for university institutions anywhere. I say "anywhere" deliberately, because one of the most remarkable features of universities is (to borrow a word from chemistry) their isomorphism. The cultural environments in (say) America, Africa, Italy, and Peru are vastly different. But go into their universities, listen to their chemistry lectures, attend their faculty board meetings, and what will strike you are the similarities, not the differences. The medieval label for a degree was *ius ubique docendi*, "the right to teach anywhere," and it is still a valid label. Any institution which disregarded this isomorphism by making changes inconsistent with essentials in the global concept of a university would find itself out of the world league, to its great misfortune.

So it becomes important to specify exactly what we mean by "inconsistent" changes, and what we mean by "essentials." What scope is there for a university to evolve without affront to its heredity? And what are the forces which propel its evolution? Let me answer the second question first. Universities have three categories of customers: the students, the employers of graduates, and, in a state university, the legislature representing the public who foot the bill. All three of these categories of customers have legitimate claims on the university. They constitute three forces which act upon the administration, often in contrary directions. Student pressure may be for expansion; pressure from the legislature may be for economy; pressure from employers may be for what they consider to be the "right kind" of graduates. The pressures are often capricious and they are liable to change direction in unpredictable ways. Who, for instance, at the time of the sputnik scare could have foretold that barely ten years later there would be an embarrassing superfluity of Ph.D.'s in science and technology? A university which disregarded the pressures would soon find itself at loggerheads with its own community. The art of university administration is to receive this continual feedback from the customers, to distinguish between what the scientist describes as "messages" and what he describes as "background noise," and to devise policies which respond to the messages in ways which are consistent with the inner logic of the university — that is to say with the hereditary nature which it shares with universities all over the world. This art of administration calls for a continual resolution of conflicts between pressures for change and resistance due to constitutional inertia. The inertia is commonly criticised as academic mulishness. Inertia is in fact an essential attribute, for it confers stability on the institution and gives the administrator time to work out the profit and loss of the changes being pressed upon him. It is, or at any rate it should be, an inertia built from principles and it should command the consensus of the academic community.

Let us now turn to the first of the two questions I asked: What scope is there for change within the constraints of tradition? One way to answer this question is to decide which features of tradition are worth preserving and which are superfluous or anachronistic. I can illustrate this by recalling the way British universities were exported to tropical Africa in the 1950's. The college in Ghana in those days (it is different now) was a caricature of a Cambridge college. The faculty, adorned in gowns, walked in procession into the dining hall to sit at a high table on a raised dais; students, also adorned in gowns, stood as a gong was sounded; a Latin grace was read; waiters in uniform served the meal; and afterwards the faculty retired again in procession to the Common Room where they drank port wine at a temperature of eighty-five degrees and endeavoured to hold highbrow conversation. (And, lest this incident be dismissed as a piece of British complacency for which there is no American parallel, let me add in parenthesis that I recall also another African university, sponsored by an American institution, which was a facsimile, planted in the African bush, of a Middle-west land-grant college, complete with a gigantic stadium, tomato ketchup and metal boxes of paper napkins on the cafeteria tables, and those uniquely American triangular pennants adorning the rooms of the dormitories.)

Mimicry of tradition like this is trivial and sometimes ludicrous. But let us have another look at the college in Ghana in the 1950's. It was affiliated to the University of London, one of the great universities of the world. Every year a swarm of examiners flew out from England to take part in the assessment of candidates for degrees. A bachelor of arts from Ghana in those days had pursued courses of study and passed examinations indistinguishable in quality from those in London itself. His degree was on the gold standard of learning. This uncompromising insistence on academic standards was not achieved without opposition; there were people who maintained that a developing country with a poor high school system should not aspire to a high standard for its graduates. After all (they said) the standard of a pass degree at Oxford or Cambridge in the nineteenth century was derisory; African universities, too, could start modestly and step up standards later. Fortunately the opposition was overruled. But in the 1850's, when Britain exported universities to India, there was no insistence on academic standards. The first failure rates were so high that the pass marks were relaxed. Indian universities have never recovered from this mistake; of course their graduates include men and women of the highest intelligence, but Indian degrees are no trustworthy measure of ability and their currency on the academic market remains dubious. In the 1950's, when Britain exported universities to Africa, she did not repeat this mistake. As a result, graduates from Nigeria or Ghana or Kenya know that their degrees are legal academic tender anywhere in the world.

In African universities (in both former British and French colonies) the tradition of a world currency for the degree has not been breached. But within this tradition there has been scope for change. The content of curricula, for example, can be altered without sacrificing standards. History, as originally taught in these African colonial colleges, followed slavishly the syllabus in London. Graduates could write glibly about Tudor England but were pathetically ignorant on the history of their own nation. (One distinguished African scholar who proposed to put on a course of Nigerian history was told by the British professor who was chairman of the department that there was no such subject!) After some resistance from people who seemed incapable of distinguishing the difference between standard of achievement and content of syllabus, the African universities were permitted to design indigenous curricula which were still accepted by the University of London as ingredients for its degrees. One consequence of this in the field of history is that African scholarship has flourished; in universities all over the world African studies now take an honourable place beside studies of Europe and the Americas.

So, to come back to my theme, the constraints of tradition, at any rate as we see them in Britain, require a university to nurture intellectual excellence and to be implacably opposed to any cheapening of its degree, for this is the unique function of a university which no other institution can perform. The functions of a research institute, intellectual service station, social finishing school, could be performed elsewhere; but a mastery of intellectual systems, nowhere else. However, within these constraints there is plenty of room for innovation and change. Purists like Abraham Flexner have ridiculed the inclusion of such subjects as educational psychology and biolinguistics in the curriculum of American universities as unworthy to stand in the same course list as classics, mathematics, or philosophy. But this is mere intellectual snobbery. All curricula reforms have had to be driven through barriers erected by pedants. Listen to an Oxford don, writing in 1849: "I can but fear the worst, a majority of 14 in convocation voted in favour of . . . Modern History. We did indeed by a large majority reject the details of this novelty, but the principle has been admitted. . . . [W]e have fallen into the weakness of yielding to the spirit of the age." It has taken us a long time to learn that a liberal education (as Samuel Alexander wrote) is a spirit of pursuit, not a choice of subject.

But, some will say, what I have just written about excellence is also intellectual snobbery. It is to equate university education with an elitist tradition, and that is inconsistent with the commitment in America and in Britain to mass higher education. It is true that until comparatively recently universities were designed for very small minority groups; sometimes for minorities with brains, sometimes for minorities with money. The whole idea of mass higher education has, therefore, to be reconciled to the university tradition, for if it were irreconcilable, the idea would have to be resisted. "More means worse," the critics say. Without doubt more means different. But worse? I do not think so. It has been proved on the campuses of great American universities that excellence and mediocrity can coexist, sharing the same dormitories and cafeterias and central heating plants. Even those sanctuaries of elitism, Oxford and Cambridge, nurtured until quite recently agreeable and moneyed boneheads alongside the most brilliant intellects of the nation. The mathematical genius and the hearty oarsman lived on the same college staircase. Oxford and Cambridge are not like that today; entry is now highly meritocratic, but I doubt whether the intellectual climate is any more stimulating than it used to be.

Most of us have come to the conclusion that there is nothing illogical about a multipurpose university, provided the priorities among the purposes are consistent with its unique function. In an age (if such an age ever existed) when universities had nothing to offer except opportunities to read, to reflect, to search for truth — with no promise of social advancement, no prospect of higher pay — they could pursue their limited function in tranquility, free from pressures from a world which was simply not interested in them. Although we now live in a very different age, this function — a partnership of teachers and scholars engaged in the detached and disinterested study of intellectual systems — remains the generic characteristic of a university. Every nation needs to have some institutions where this is the first priority. But universities have for a long time been the victims of their own success. It is now recognised that the study of intellectual systems supports the whole structure of modern society. Universities, therefore, find themselves in the embarrassing position of holding a monopoly. To enter the professions, to rise in the social scale, to acquire power: these aspirations nowadays are difficult to fulfil without a higher education. Almost the only kind of worldly success which is independent of the university monopoly is moneymaking. So practically everyone now wants a college degree and the phrase "mass higher education" has come to represent a sort of human right.

Universities simply have to live with this attitude. It is part of the price they have to pay for being "kept" by society, and it is no bad thing. Just as Henry Ford gave access to the American countryside for millions who could not afford Rolls Royce automobiles, so the state universities have given access to the world of learning for millions who would not have been capable or desirous of reaching the esoteric standards of Oxford or Harvard. But the analogy of automobiles must not be carried too far. The American university system differs from the automobile assembly line in a very important respect: the "Rolls Royce" and the "Ford" scholars (to their mutual benefit) share the same campus. Gresham's law does not operate: the modest degree does not drive out the elite degree; indeed it is only because public demand for the modest degree is satisfied that the elite degree can hold its standard. So, in dealing with academic standards, the path of reconciliation of tradition with modernity is to arrange for their coexistence without diluting the thin clear stream of excellence which produces tomorrow's intellectual leaders. Fortunately this thin clear stream is not monopolised by the few elite institutions; it may occur anywhere, and anywhere it occurs it has to be cherished.

I asserted just now that a university's first priority remains the detached study of intellectual systems. This is certainly the conviction of the mandarinate who constitute the community of scholars. But it is disputed by students and employers of graduates. Students are demanding (though they put it more crudely than this) that intellectual systems be linked to human systems. By "human systems" I do not mean the conventional rational study of man as it is to be found in courses on economics, sociology, and anthropology; these I regard as intellectual systems. I mean the matrix of cognitive and noncognitive values within which personal and political judgements are made. How to include this element of the affective in an environment dedicated to reason poses the most perplexing problem of reconciling tradition and modernity in universities. To reject this demand outright, to maintain that the terms of discourse in a university should be confined to the objective and the rational, is commonly justified as a legitimate defence of the academic tradition. It is nothing of the kind, for, throughout most of their long history, universities have been religious foundations, where detached scholarship was permeated by faith in immaterial, affective values. These values, in turn, determined the norms for morality, ethics, and interpersonal relations. Human systems, which were codified in spiritual doctrine (not all of it rational) underpinned intellectual systems which were codified in rational thought. With the coming of secular universities this spiritual foundation was weakened. For a few generations the social and moral pillars of the foundation survived. We call it the Protestant ethic. That, too, is now showing signs of decay. This association of the higher learning with religion is a world-wide phenomenon. Medieval universities took their authority from the pope, and long before the invention of universities there were other institutions of higher learning, also based on religions: the madrasas — a millennium old — of the Muslim world; the Buddhist college at Taxila in India, which was flourishing under the Emperor Asoka in the third century B.C. Even in the remote and supposedly primitive city of Timbuctoo there was, in the sixteenth century, an academy of learning. One aphorism from it has been preserved: "Salt from the north, gold from the south, and silver from the white man's country; but the word of God and the treasures of wisdom are to be found in Timbuctoo."

So the university administrator has to face this question: Does it matter that one of the ancient traditional features of universities, the association of intellectual systems with human and spiritual systems, is disappearing; and if it does matter, what should take its place? There is growing evidence that it does matter. First, the students complain. It is not that they want the churches to take charge of universities again. For many of them organised religion has lost credibility too; they reject its dogmatism, its authoritarianism, its cant. What they do want is assurance that scholarly detachment can be reconciled with social concern. They want the whole style of teaching and learning to reflect this reconciliation. They discern that many of those who teach them have suffered their own social concern to atrophy, under pressure of the analytical attitude necessary for the pursuit of scholarship. So when academics protest that universities are not competent to impart anything except the scholarly virtues, they have a strong case. The campus is well equipped to deal with intellectual systems, but poorly equipped to deal with human systems. Nevertheless, when you set aside the strident empty rhetoric of student protest, the thoughtless non-negotiable demands, the flashes of emotional involvement alternating with apathy, something significant remains. The students (the university's most important customers) include many who are disenchanted with aseptic intellectual systems. And they can claim venerable support for their disenchantment. No less a man than A. N. Whitehead wrote: "It is an erroneous moral platitude, that it is necessarily good to know the truth. The minor truth may beget the major evil."

But it is not only the students who complain; employers complain too. For the great majority of graduates will not become scholars (where concern with human systems might not matter much); they will go out into a world where decision-making begins with data, rational thought, and objective analysis, but where those are not the final end; they are only the first step of the process. The next step is the linking of intellectual systems with human systems: with the electorate, the customer, the patient, the client, the employee. And the graduate may find (if he is a graduate from an English university, he *will* find) that there is precious little he has learnt at college which will help him to understand how to link intellectual systems with human systems, or even to realise that a link is necessary.

Recently (in January 1974) a whole page of the London *Times* was occupied by an advertisement signed by twenty-eight leaders in industry and business, declaring that in recruiting men into business management in their firms they would recognise three years' service as an army officer as equivalent to three years at a university (the normal length of a bachelor course in England). This is a good advertisement for the army, but it does, or should, confront universities with a sharp challenge. Are employers seeking qualities like loyalty, leadership, power to command (or its obverse: willingness to accept leadership and to obey), capacity to handle people in trying situations, and ability to get on with men of very diverse educational backgrounds, rather than the qualities which a college education confers: capacity to master data, familiarity with intellectual systems and the symbols in which the systems are expressed, the habit of regarding issues with detachment, discarding their irrational elements, and a predilection to challenge orthodoxy and to dispute tradition? Or (a more sensitive question) are we in English universities not equipping our students with these scholarly qualities anyway, while a military training does equip men with the other qualities?

At all events, two of the customers of universities, students and employers, include people who, for different reasons, are not satisfied that universities should confine their interests to intellectual systems: the students, because there is developing among them what Clark Kerr calls "new mentalities . . . a new interest in the affective and the sensate"; and the employers, because they are obliged to depend on universities as their main source of recruits for generalist jobs, the jobs requiring personality and character more than specialist expertise. These are powerful pressures upon the university administration. The response to them (to come back to my theme) must be consistent with what is essential in the academic tradition. Undoubtedly a failure to respond to the pressures would be *inconsistent* with the essentials, because for seven out of their eight centuries of history universities did in fact graft intellectual systems on to a religion which subsumed human systems. To restore concern for human systems would be no new thing. But there are massive difficulties in deciding the strategy of response. Let me begin by specifying some responses which would surely be damaging to higher education. First, universities which are secular should not abandon their secular status. There are, of course, some universities and colleges in the world which adhere to the old tradition: their membership is frankly for professing Catholics, or Calvinists, or Buddhists, or Jews. But to impose on a secular institution the dogma of any religious faith, or any rigid and arbitrary code of morality except the morality inherent in scholarship itself, would be to invite protest or hypocrisy. Second, universities are severely damaged if they succumb to corporate commitment in political issues, unless the issues (such as apartheid in South Africa) infringe the freedom of the university itself. There are still a few mischievous and misguided people who dispute this assertion. I use the words "mischievous and misguided" deliberately, because any such corporate commitment, unless it is unanimously supported by all members of the corporation, diminishes the freedom of those members who may dissent from it. And diminution of freedom is intolerable, even for the political activists themselves. Third, any concession to the "new interest in the affective and the sensate" should not be at the expense of the rational and cognitive, for that remains the chief business of the university. Where the university can contribute, and contribute legitimately, to the new need generated by mass higher education is in making links between intellectual and human systems.

Let me put it another way. It would (I hope) be agreed by all who are concerned with universities that it is their business to *educate*, not just to *instruct*. An educated (as contrasted with a merely instructed) citizen is expected to have three capacities or skills: some skill with ideas, some skill with things, some skill with people. In some countries (Britain is an example) skill with ideas is regarded as the special function of the university, and skill with things is regarded as the special function of the polytechnics and technical colleges. American universities offer opportunities to acquire both these skills.

But skill with people? That happy tact which prevents confrontation between two sides in a dispute; that flair for mobilising support for a policy; the cultivation of "antennae" that enable the statesman, the leader, the administrator, the arbitrator, to gauge public opinion and to react to it; that capacity for interpreting the hard data in the context of human happiness and welfare: where can these skills be acquired? Not, I think, in universities on either side of the Atlantic. Of course the "mix" of skills required for different walks of life is very different. A mathematical genius can get along with the minimum capacity for dealing with things and people. A salesman — and, one suspects, alas! a politician — needs a high capacity for dealing with people but can get by with a very modest capacity for dealing with ideas. The contemporary problem in universities can be put very simply. They are institutions which specialise in skill with ideas, but most of the graduates they produce nowadays are likely to need, as their main achievement, a capacity to deal with people. It was an ex-university president who said that university administration was no great strain on the intellect, but a great strain on the character; and this is true not only of university administration. In a world spinning in precarious equilibrium skill with people is the supreme stabiliser. Can universities afford to leave this skill out of the curriculum?

It is a skill best learnt, no doubt, "on the job"; indeed there are some who say it cannot be learnt any other way. I dispute this. Something can be done within the framework of formal college education. But it has to be done judiciously. Learning to link intellectual systems with human systems must not be a soft option, wrapped in woolly generalisations. What can be done at college level is to introduce the student to the exhausting exercise of deciding between two policies, neither of which is supported by *all* the rational arguments, and either of which will benefit some people and harm others. A good example of this exercise is decision-making over the control of pollution. Consider a specific case. The dedicated conservationist wants clean rivers. The community wants cheap food. In one study of the river-polluting effluent from a sugar beet factory (cited in the second annual report of the Council on Environmental Quality, 1971) it was calculated that up to 30 percent of the pollutant could be removed at a marginal cost of about ninety cents per pound; but to remove (say) 80 percent of the pollutant would put the marginal cost up to about thirty-six dollars per pound of pollutant removed. The choice is on one hand a cleaner river and a higher price for sugar from the factory, on the other hand a dirtier river and cheaper sugar. A balance has to be struck between two benefits and two diseconomies. Hard data and rational argument help to illuminate the problem to be solved; but

 40666

North Carolina Wesleyan College Libr
Rocky Mount, North Carolina 27801

there comes a moment when a decision has to be made which will depend not on logic alone, but on hunch. To take students through case histories of this kind (one can think of many more: the Alaska pipeline, phosphates in detergents, DDT) is an illuminating experience. It does not, of course, replace the affective element in a religious tradition, but it does bring home to the student that there is no antithesis between rational thought and social concern: the most down-to-earth decisions rest on ethical considerations as well as logic.

A modest but effective aim in this sort of education would be to equip the student to distinguish between the art of decision-making in pure science and scholarship (which, I repeat, must remain the university's prime concern) and the art of decision-making in society. There are three important differences. The first is the time factor. For the scholar there is no deadline except the one he sets for himself. If more experiments are needed, if another document has to be seen before the question can be answered, the scholar simply postpones publication; he can, if he likes, delay a decision until he has all the relevant data, even if they take years to collect. With the man of affairs it is otherwise. He works to a deadline; by such-and-such a day the decision has to be taken, whether there is enough information or not. Second, the scholar's decisions are usually reversible. If the experiment fails to answer the question, he scraps it and designs another one. If the hypothesis is inconsistent with the facts, the hypothesis is jettisoned. The man of affairs, by contrast, may find himself making irreversible decisions. The route of a highway, the siting of an airport: once decisions about these are made, there are permanent "second order" social consequences which can never be put into reverse. Third, the scientist and scholar set their own objectives for their work; their business is not only to answer questions: it is also to invent the questions. So the *ends* of academic studies are not controversial; they are self-determined. By contrast again, the *ends* in political decisions may be as controversial as the *means*, and they are determined by forces the decision-maker cannot control.

These very simple examples illustrate the paradox which Alvin Weinberg has vividly described: "In the university the specialist and analyst is king. . . . In society the non-specialist and synthesiser is king." The function of modern universities is to educate a few specialists and a great many nonspecialists. For the former function they are well equipped. For the latter function they are not. The training and the proclivity of the faculty are, naturally, toward discipline-oriented patterns of thought. (This is true even for the style of approach to technology and the social sciences.) The great majority of graduates will go into an environment where they need to use problem-oriented patterns of thought. These require a style of approach which can link intellectual systems to human systems. My modest contribution to these essays is to suggest one way in which this style of approach might be included in the curriculum.

Brand Blanshard

Democracy and Distinction in American Education

My subject today is the dilemma of our higher education. It is a dilemma so fundamental as to form a philosophical as well as a practical problem. Two ideals, both of them essential parts of the American way of thinking, seem to be in conflict with each other. One is the ideal of democracy, of equal rights for all. The other is the ideal of individual distinction. And the difficulty is that the more democratic education becomes, the less it favors such distinction; and the more it raises and refines its standards, the less democratic it becomes. Throw open the doors of colleges and universities to all who want to come, and we no longer have higher education, for, as Professor Douglas Bush puts it, "education for all is education for none." On the other hand, lift education to a level where it is genuinely exacting, and you close the doors to the great majority. In education there seems to be an inverse variation between democracy and distinction. Quantity is at war with quality.

I do not think we can afford to lose either the democratic ideal of our education or our hope for quality, and I want to consider with you how to deal with the dilemma. But first let us see the two sides a little more clearly.

What do we mean by democracy? Its root Greek meaning is the rule of the people. Democracy came into being as a protest against the rule over the many by a privileged and powerful few, and the protest sprang from the conviction that this special privilege was wrong because men were in some sense equal. Equality is the kernel of democracy. But equality in what sense? Certainly not equality in fact, for we are not born with the same genes. I can never hope to equal Muhammad Ali, or Bobby Fischer, or Charlie Chaplin, or Mark Spitz, or Pablo Casals. Is the equality implied by democracy then equality of opportunity? No again, for such equality is not really possible. We may throw open the college doors to the young Einsteins in our high schools and to the youngsters who sit in a cloud of unknowing beside them, but in so doing we are not offering them opportunities that are really equal. To the clouded mind a textbook of algebra will remain forever a closed book, and an opportunity of which the student cannot take advantage is not for him an opportunity at all. Among the inequalities with which nature brings us into the world is the inequality in our capacity to use the opportunities extended to us, and that inequality is past all remedy.

No, the equality implied by democracy is neither equality of gifts nor equality of opportunity, but equality of consideration. My arm may be feeble and my brain equally so, but still I am a person, with my own aspirations and my own capacity for suffering, and when the privileges of society are distributed, I must not be left out; my good must be taken into account; I have an equal right with anyone else to have my needs and aims considered. The story is told that Sir James Barrie was walking an Edinburgh street one winter's day in a mood of abstraction and almost bumped into a stranger who, by quickly stepping aside, avoided a collision. When Barrie turned round apologetically, the stranger was standing and looking at him reproachfully. "God made me too," he said. The stranger turned out to be Robert Louis Stevenson, and the encounter began a lifelong friendship. But what interests me at the moment is that that remark of Stevenson is the ultimate reply of the democrat to anyone who would push him around. I may be queer and soiled and seedy, but here I am, a living soul like you, with hopes and pains as real as yours. "God made me too."

Such equality, I think, is the essential meaning of democracy. To the great credit of America, we have tried to embody it in our educational system, and we have done so with an immense burst of energy in the past few decades. A fit of conscience on the part of administrations has coincided with a surge of ambition in the younger populace to form the longest queues in history in front of our college gates. Today it is widely believed that if anyone is to cope adequately with our complex age he needs a college education. And if it would promote both his own good and that of society to have it, does not society owe it to him and he have a right to it? In a recent *Bulletin* of the Association of University Professors we find an article called "The Case for Universal Higher Education" in which the author says: "The drive to make higher education universal will not be spent until the same proportion of the population holds a college degree as presently holds a high school diploma."

This line of thought, like an ascending rocket, is likely to burst into astonishing fragments in the way of conclusions. If education is a right and not to grant it is discrimination, then it is wrong for university authorities to discriminate among applicants, and we find City College of New York throwing open its gates to anyone who has survived the grades. The argument is applied from the bottom up. Children must not only be admitted equally to schools; they must be treated equally once they get there. In a discussion of pupil differences, a teacher writes: "I regard it as undemocratic to treat so-called gifted children any differently from other children. To me all children are gifted." And a respected educator says: "Any school system in which one child may fail while another succeeds is unjust, undemocratic, and uneducational." [1] So pupils are advanced a grade a year regardless of failure; what must be avoided is the *sense* of failure. College students, as one might expect, have greeted this form of the argument with enthusiasm. Are you really treating them equally if you discriminate among them in ability? There have been movements in many colleges to abolish grades as undemocratic. My own college of Yale, where I began my teaching with a razor-sharp system of grading on a scale of one hundred, first changed to Honors, Pass, and Fail, then to A-B-C-D-E-F, and then dropped that outrageously undemocratic and discriminatory F from the student's public record. Student protests on behalf of democracy have led in some colleges to the inclusion of undergraduates on the boards of trustees and to the revision of the curriculum to meet their current interests. By a natural extension, the idea of democracy among persons has led to the idea of democracy among subjects. If the elective system is right in principle, why should it not be followed consistently? Why should there be a pecking order among subjects of study? Why should a student be compelled to take German or French when he wants to take Swahili, or to study "the dismal science," economics, if he is more interested in interior decorating or pottery? Not that student pressures for democracy are always self-interested; they may be generous to the point of masochism. Students are not only giving up their fraternities and sororities as unjust to those who are not elected; some of them are turning back their Phi Beta Kappa keys on the ground that honor societies are necessarily undemocratic.

These are a few straws in the democratic breeze blowing through the academic groves. Now for the opposite trend. To many thoughtful persons higher education seems in its idea and essence to exclude

---

[1] The two quotations are given in John W. Gardner, *Excellence* (New York: Harper, 1961), pp. 74–75 and 112. The second comes originally from Marietta Louise Johnson, *Youth in a World of Men: The Child, the Parent, and the Teacher* (New York: John Day, 1929), p. 13.

democracy, to make a general extension of its privileges impossible. Those privileges are really open only to the few who can take advantage of them. In this sense, higher education is and must be elitist. To be sure, this has been questioned, like everything else in education. If one holds that the mind is a tabula rasa, as Locke did, a blank page on which the only writing is that of experience, education can make anything of anyone; that is why a good empiricist like John Stuart Mill could hold that any normal boy or girl in England could have produced all that he had in logic, political economy, and metaphysics, if only that child had been in the charge of James Mill, John Stuart's formidable father. But Mill's empiricism, I take it, is as dead as Lysenko's biology, which was another attempt to make nurture prevail over nature.

The elitist in education is not necessarily a snob; he may have his feet planted firmly on experimental fact. Psychologists have devoted an almost infinite ingenuity to devising tests for every human faculty, and they have found — what indeed was evident enough to any reflective schoolteacher — that in all these faculties our native capital varies from near zero to the sky. Take our visualizing powers. There have been painters with a visual imagery so vivid that they have been able to continue painting from a sitter's image the day after he has left; there are also persons who are puzzled as to what you can mean by speaking of a mental image at all. Take memory. Professor Billy Phelps of Yale liked to tell of his brother Dryden Phelps, who could call up what he had been doing on any date you mentioned in the past forty years, and to contrast him with the helpless man who complained that there were three things he never could remember: "I can't remember names, I can't remember faces, and — dear me, I can't remember the third thing I can't remember." Now it is nonsense, says the nativist, to say that this variation of achievement is due to experience or practice; it is clearly the by-product of one's genes.

Some people can do, without practice, what others could never do with any amount of practice.

Among these variable faculties is a peculiarly fundamental one — intelligence. Intelligence has been variously defined. Sometimes it is the power to grasp things in relation; sometimes it is simply the power to understand; sometimes it is the power to apply past experience to the solution of new problems. Many psychologists have now given up trying to define it and are content to say, "I mean by intelligence what my intelligence tests test." But however one defines it, if the definition is at all plausible it will stand for something both fundamental and variable in the extreme.

Now education must take account of these facts. For the man of high intelligence can profitably study calculus, economic and ethical theory, constitutional law, the principles of physics, organic chemistry, the philosophy of history, and aesthetic criticism. The man of low intelligence, defined in any plausible way, will make little or nothing of these subjects, for they all require a power to move freely among relations and abstractions that nature has not granted him. Yet it is these and other subjects like them that form the staple of higher education. To ask the man of low or even ordinary intelligence to master such subjects is not improbably to encourage a waste of time, failure, and in the end a hatred of all things academic. The inference is clear. Higher education should be reserved for the few of marked intelligence. Let the many take themselves elsewhere.

I think you will agree that there is some force in this case. Of course, like the argument for democracy, it has been carried much farther. Just as the extreme democrats want to widen the circle of those admitted to higher education, so the extreme elitists want to contract it, and sometimes on strange grounds. Oxford and Cambridge, until a labor government came into power, were aristocratic enclaves which, by their entrance examinations, their cost, and their special relations to private schools, effectively excluded practically everyone outside certain social classes. Many of our own best schools and colleges have been in effect elitist because of their tuition rates which have excluded all those below a certain level of wealth. As a high-school boy in Detroit, I wanted to go to Princeton, but I found that for one of my financial status to go to Princeton was like his going to the moon; so I went with gratitude to the University of Michigan, where the tuition was some forty dollars a year and therefore accessible through my newspaper route. Some thoughtful people are elitists not by inadvertence but by design, T. S. Eliot for example. He thought that high culture in a society was best preserved through a hereditary aristocracy. The university would reflect aristocratic conceptions and manners, and with their aid would train the leaders and set the moral and intellectual tone of the country. Eliot would have found his grandfather's notion of a free elective system among subjects most distasteful; as for himself, he made religion central in the education. In words that might have been written by Cardinal Newman, he says: "Education is from top to bottom religious, or it is not education." And "the hierarchy of education should be a religious hierarchy. The universities are too far gone in secularization." [2]

Between these two trends, the democratic and the elitist, our universities must find their way. You will agree, I think, that neither view can be accepted in its extreme form. A consistent democracy in higher education is quite impracticable. In elementary education, to be sure, it is both possible and necessary; in a society like ours the irreducible minimum of equipment for a citizen is to read, write, and count. At the high school level difficulties appear, for the wave of dropouts, partly due to apathy and bad teaching, is also partly due to an inability to master subjects of some complexity. But college for all

---

[2] Of the two quotations from Eliot the first is from *The Christian News-letter* (London), 3 September 1941, quoted in Rossell Hope Robbins, *The T. S. Eliot Myth* (New York: H. Schuman, 1951), p. 13. The second is from *Essays Ancient and Modern* (New York: Harcourt, Brace & Co., 1936), p. 183.

would mean either a brutal slaughter of the innocents in the first year or the turning of universities into high schools and a general degradation of their standards.

Elitism too, if that means preserving the privilege of higher education to any class except the academically qualified, seems out of the question in this country. In time past membership in a first family or a family of wealth would perhaps suffice to get one past the gates of the Ivy League. Ask any father of such an applicant whether that holds today, and you will get an answer that is unequivocal and perhaps explosive. The trend against reserving higher education for those of hereditary or social or financial position is strong and growing stronger.

But if neither the democratic nor the elitist view is acceptable policy, what line should we take? As usual, the wisest course seems to lie somewhere in the middle. Indeed, between a sensible democracy and a sensible elitism there need be no contradiction at all. Since I am now beyond practical responsibility in the matter, let me indulge in a bit of dogmatism about the things we must cling to in meeting the problem. If what I offer sounds like elitism, I hope it is not an undemocratic elitism.

My main contention is that we must not compromise on quality. We must keep higher education genuinely high, and raise it higher. We must not sacrifice quality to quantity, standards to standardization, the value of our degrees to the popular demand for them. We should clear our minds as to what intellectual quality means. We should not pretend that mathematics or physics is easy, or turn philosophy into the story of philosophy, or art criticism into the story of artists, or Maynard Keynes into a popularization of economics, in order that the many should get by. The main reason is that the truth in all these fields is difficult, complex, and elusive, and if it is made so simple that he who runs may read, what he is reading is almost certainly not the truth but some distortion or vulgarization of it. And even if the truth is stated with perfect lucidity, it is not something that can be passively absorbed as if it were a motion picture and the student a spectator in an easy chair. It can be understood only if the student exercises in some measure the powers that went to its discovery, the powers of reflective analysis, inference, and checking of theory against fact. The new physics is unintelligible unless one can follow quantum and relativity theory, and those laymen among us who have tried to read Heisenberg or Einstein will know with sadness what I mean. Knowledge in this century has expanded far faster than man's ability to keep up with it; the individual mind is falling farther and farther behind; the standard of competence in every field is becoming more exacting. It follows that a smaller and smaller fraction of us are able to meet that standard.

Hence to make the university a place of increasingly popular education is the reverse of the right line. It points to the lowering of standards until they are adjusted to mass capacity, since no institution could maintain itself if it consistently flunked most of its students. A university that enrolls the masses will accept mass standards, and if it does that it will no longer be an institution of higher learning. Further, it will be an anachronism. It is not requiring of the student the level of analytic and reflective power that leadership in the modern world demands.

We may expect a protest here from the educational democrats. They will say: "You are an elitist after all. You would keep university education for the few. You are arguing for standards that would exclude from such education most of those who want it and need it. You are ignoring the rights of the ordinary man who after all is in the majority and has rights to an education as truly as the genius."

It is important to be clear on this "right to education." What gives anyone a right to education, or freedom, or a vote, or anything else? A right is a duty looked at from the other end. If I have a right to freedom or education or a vote, what that means is that society has a duty to grant me that privilege. Very well, what makes it society's duty to grant anyone a privilege? Ultimately one thing only: the fact that granting it subserves the greatest good of all affected by it. Private property normally is a right because it subserves that end, but it is not always a right; we recognize that the community may, with due compensation, take my house and lot away if the public requires my ground for a needed highway.

Now does anyone have a right to education? Yes, if spending the community's money and effort in educating him would do more for the general good than another way of spending them; and most civilized communities have thought that on that ground children do have a right to the primary education that would make them literate. Do they have a right also to secondary education? Here there must be more discrimination. There is little doubt of the advantage in happiness and competence of a citizenry educated as widely as practicable through the high school level. But it is becoming increasingly plain that there are great numbers of pupils to whose needs and capacities the standard high school curriculum is unsuited. Do they have a right to be carried through it nevertheless? Or to put the same question otherwise, are we economically serving the public good when we attempt, at high cost to the public in money and to the schools in effectiveness, to educate the relatively uneducable? The question must at least give us pause. And when it is repeated at the university level the answer is surely No.

The rights at this level lie in another quarter. We have become so accustomed to thinking of rights exclusively in terms of the disadvantaged that we tend to forget the even stronger rights of the naturally advantaged. It is to the potential leaders of the next generation that in reality we owe the most. It is by recognizing them early, by selecting them for special attention, by giving them the stimulus and environment that will elicit their powers to the full that we shall get the richest return on our educational investment. And for this stimulus and this environment we must rely on the universities. Our universities are not parade grounds for the millions in our educational ranks, but schools specially equipped to train the officers in the continuing joint war against ignorance, insecurity, and injustice. We are not neglecting the many in thus favoring the few. It is no service to the many to smother their potential leaders in educational mediocrity on the way to their posts of leadership. The few can raise the level of the many. The many cannot raise the level of the few except in one way. By seeing to it that the few have the chance to reach their highest level of leadership and competence, the many will raise their own level too.

Sometimes what is not obvious in the abstract becomes so in the concrete. Suppose you are a high school teacher in Ogden, Utah, with money at your disposal for a scholarship that will send one of your pupils, and only one, to the University of Utah. Most of your pupils are John Does — run-of-the-mill, healthy, pink-cheeked young Americans, keen about the band and the high school teams, their science a C−, their history a C+, and their English a mess in B minor. None of them looks like university material. But in the four corners of your classroom — and here I must call on your imagination — are four unusual types. Bulging from one corner seat there is a magnificent brute of a fellow named Jim Thorpe, perhaps less than outstanding in his schoolwork, but a whole football squad and track team in himself. In another corner there is a spidery young imp named Bertrand Russell, who amuses himself by correcting the teacher's equations. In the third corner there is a dainty damsel named Marilyn Monroe, who is in difficulties in social studies but is a twinkling star in social practice and who can choose among thirty invitations to every dance. In the fourth corner there is a bright, argumentative Jewish boy named Walter Lippmann, who is no use at games but is the mainstay of the debating team. Which of the class would you choose? I suspect you would by-pass the John Does. I suspect too that there are scholarship committees who would succumb in awe to young Thorpe and would be melted into marshmallows by Miss Monroe. But I must add that if they sent either of these latter candidates to the university in preference to either of the others, they would betray both the candidates and the community. Send up Doe or Thorpe or Monroe, and your candidate will gasp in history and go under finally in symbolic logic. Send up Russell, and he will take in hand the science of logic and reconstruct it from its foundations. Send up Lippmann, and he will become one of the shrewdest counselors of his generation on every aspect of public policy. If we talk about right to education, it is to people like these that we must give our priorities. As John W. Gardner has said, "Everyone does not have a right to be a college graduate, any more than everyone has a right to run a four-minute mile." There are times, as Irving Babbitt noted, when we should "seek to substitute the right man for the doctrine of the rights of man."

If we pass over the Does, Thorpes, and Monroes in favor of the Russells and the Lippmanns, it is on the ground of an assumption which should be brought clearly to light. The assumption is a fundamental one regarding the purpose of a university. We are assuming that the purpose of a university is not to produce halfbacks or beauty queens — or, we may add, butchers, bakers, or moneymakers — but what? Woodrow Wilson answered this by saying: "The object of the University is singly and entirely intellectual." Dr. Hutchins answered by saying: "The task of education is to make rational minds more perfectly rational." Alexander Meiklejohn answered by saying: "The college, as a place of general teaching, has one aim, and that aim is intelligence." All these distinguished educators are saying essentially the same thing. When we suggest that the business of a university is with the Russells and the Lippmanns rather than with the Does, Thorpes, or Monroes, we are assuming that these educators are right, that the purpose of a university is to turn out intelligent and rational minds.

This view is bound to arouse suspicion in some quarters. The intellectual has had a rather bad press. He is sometimes thought of as a harmless and wizened little creature who enjoys his singular diet of cactus — a person who, lacking common sympathy and common sense, sits by preference in a corner spinning webs and solving puzzles, a cerebrum throbbing in a vacuum. But those who hold that the purpose of a university is intellectual would of course not admit that this creature is in their sense an intellectual at all. The business of the intellect, the reason, the intelligence of man is not the spinning of capricious webs but the understanding of the world it lives in. Reason is the interpreting, connecting, organizing function of the mind; its aim is to see things in perspective, for only so can one understand them. Reason is the main enemy of parochialism and triviality and alienation from things human. The central drive of the intellect is from facts to the laws that illuminate and explain them, and from such laws to that system of laws in which a final explanation would consist.

One must protest in passing against the common idea that the end of education is range of interest, information, or learning, however important these may be. A Yale teacher I have mentioned, William Lyon Phelps, remarked: "A very simple test that one can apply to oneself to discover a range of interest is take up the daily newspaper and see if there is something on every page of interest: foreign news, national news, local news, athletics, the theatre, music, books, stock exchange, etc., and if there is something on every page that interests a man, he is very much alive." Well, so he probably is, but his *intelligence* may not be very alive nevertheless. The mark of such intelligence is not the number of items he is acquainted with, but whether he sees their bearing on each other, whether he understands how the foreign news affects the stock reports, what is the scale of values behind the theatre, the music, and the books, and whether these values are what they ought to be. The rational man is neither a water-

spider darting about on the surface nor a mole burrowing in his
esoteric specialty. He is a man of common sense–plus, which means
that his judgment on particular issues is weighty because of the mass
of reflectively organized knowledge that speaks through it.

There are those who would agree with all this about the primacy
of intellect in higher education, but would insist that intellect has to
do with facts and relations only, and has nothing to do with standards
in the theatre or art gallery, in music or in morals. Intellect, they say,
is value-free, and if the aim of the university is intellectual, it should
not set itself up as a proponent or arbiter of values. I am convinced
that this is a mistake. A few moments ago I linked our rights and
duties with the production of the largest good. Is what makes anything good — *King Lear*, a Brahms waltz, the insight of the scientist
or the philosopher — simply the fact that people like it? Some of the
leading thinkers of the past generation have said essentially that —
Russell, Ayer, Carnap, Reichenbach; and some of the most influential anthropologists —Westermarck, Mead, Benedict, for example —
have held to a cultural relativism that is somewhat similar: If the
Greeks liked their way of doing things and some aboriginal tribes of
the Pacific liked theirs, it is idle to say that either culture is really
better than the other.

Of course these writers do not keep to this doctrine when making
their own judgments about good and evil; Russell argued eloquently
for the blessings of peace, though his theory excluded such argument
as irrelevant, and Westermarck talked of progress in a way to which
no cultural relativist is entitled. Even while proscribing the appeal
to reason, they made that appeal because they could not help it. And
so of the rest of us. *De gustibus non disputandum est*; but everyone
does dispute about taste and morals from pornography to Watergate.
And we should not dispute in this way unless we believed, at least
implicitly, that even in these vexed issues there was a true and a false,
a right and a wrong, to be discovered by clear thinking. We may

appeal here from Philip drunk to Philip sober. This universal implicit conviction is, I think, sound.

If it really is sound, the university may well take note of it. The function of the university is to support and promote the reign of reason, and reason does not stop with facts; the judgment of values also is a judgment of reason, well or ill instructed. In this age of technology there is a tendency on the part of humanists either to apologize for their unscientific disciplines or to try with dreary results to make them scientific. The apologies are uncalled for. To be sure, the scientists and technologists supply the means to the ends of our society, but it is the humanists who weigh and appraise those ends. The universities get the cream of the American crop, the young people who are to be the leaders of tomorrow. Is it not as important that such leaders should be competent judges of the values of our society, of the prevailing standards in "the media," in literature, and in morals, as that they should know their physics and economics? Matthew Arnold thought that university study should acquaint one with "the best that has been thought and said in the world," and that anyone acquainted with the best would have a touchstone by which he could tell good work from bad. Are our students being supplied with that sort of touchstone?

Their performance in recent years leaves one uncertain. Apart from an interest in peace and in justice to minorities, about which they have been generously enthusiastic, their course seems to have lacked an inner compass. They have combined, for example, a liking for the great music of the past with a liking for deafening barrages of decibels, an intellectual skepticism with a gullible credulousness toward oriental mysticism and the cruder kinds of religious evangelism, the cult of Eliot with the cult of Ginsberg, an insistence on doing one's own thing with the mass hypnotism of Woodstock, an exaltation of love with a casual sex adventurism, a concern about social realities with an escape into the unreal world of drugs.

The students of the past decade have developed a skepticism about their society's values that is not wholly baseless. They saw their country and themselves involved, on the dubious ground of national security, in a war on the other side of the world that cost more than forty thousand of their young lives. Recently they have seen their government involved in a domestic scandal whose slimy trails have led in many directions and seem to have no ends. While this is happening at the top, equally disquieting things are happening at the bottom. One after another, the larger American cities are falling under a pall of insecurity and fear as their centers become vast ghettos seething with resentment. Minority groups, convinced that they are being held down by the majority, are moved to pay them back in kind, scouting the law and treating its officers not as protectors but as enemies; "kill the cops" is a common cry. The university community, torn between compassion and anger, has itself become divided, with most unacademic epithets flying in faculty meetings.

These divisions may be merely part of a transient episode, but they may also be more. They may be the outward rash of a deep disease, a fundamental standardlessness. Thousands of students appear to be "alienated" — a favorite word now — from their society, but with nowhere to go, since they lack the moral measuring rods that would give them commitments of any stability. So they drift, sometimes into short-lived communes, sometimes into experimental marriages, usually also short-lived, sometimes into the drug culture. I know some of these youths and like them, but there were not many of them about in my youth and I don't understand them as I wish I did. They seem to be a curious combination of conformity with an anarchic, groping individualism. They are conformists in their readiness to be swept along in the latest currents of youth culture, individualists in their passionate desire to be something distinct and different. A friend of mine who has seen more of them than I have complains that in working with them it is hard to arrive at any concerted result, since each youth brings his own view, voices it, and goes away with the same opinion still; their very conformity calls for self-assertion, though neither has much depth. One is reminded of the little girl who announced herself a Unitarian and when asked what Unitarians believed, said: "We Unitarians don't believe anything. We wait to hear what other people say, and then we say 'We don't believe that'." I read occasionally a magazine about which I like everything but its name, which is *Dissent*. It is significant that in the atmosphere of today dissent as such, regardless of what is dissented from, should seem admirable.

Against this tendency of our students and society to fly into a conformity without principle and an individualism without individuality, the educated community should exert a steady resistance. The blight of American life is its growing skepticism and anarchy about values. If we are to accept as really good that which each man finds good in his own sight, then everything is good, which means equally that nothing is. It is no doubt a kind of democracy among values to say that nothing is really better than anything else, but it is less democracy than nihilism. And if, instead, democracy in this field means the rule of the majority, then we must be prepared, in television for example, to place "I Love Lucy" as Number 1 and "The Spoils of Poynton" or "The Forsyte Saga" as Number 15. Equality among values is in effect a contradictory notion, since the point of recognizing values at all is to distinguish better from worse; and to make people's judgments of equal weight ends in absurdity. If "we needs must love the highest when we see it," we needs must also have trained eyes and a trained mind if we are to see it at all.

I believe myself that judgments of goodness and beauty are in the end rational judgments which are true or false and defensible by reason, though this is not the place or time to state my case. I know that there are many students and some distinguished existentialist theologians who are in frank revolt against reason as one of the idols from which they want to be emancipated. But most of the great moralists have thought that emancipation from reason was not freedom but surrender to feeling and impulse, which was itself a form of slavery. This lesson, taught by the main tradition in ethics from the Greeks down, we have not managed to transmit to our students; and to anyone who holds that the purpose of the university is to advance the claims of the rational life that must be a matter of concern. Is it really visionary to ask that the university, which stands for the appeal to reason in science, should also stand for rational guidance in the sphere of values? I am only following a long line of philosophers and educators in holding that there are rational standards not only in logic, but in art and letters and life as well, and that these standards are accessible to those who reflectively seek them. Perhaps if we university teachers had done our job more effectively in exemplifying and transmitting them, our students would not have been seduced so readily into wandering after false gods.

The case for the university as the citadel of rationality in thought, feeling, and practice is the stronger because the general public in this country has traditionally mistrusted and misunderstood the intellectual. If one doubts that, a glance at Richard Hofstadter's admirable book *Anti-Intellectualism in American Life* will open one's eyes. We sometimes think of America, as did H. A. L. Fisher, the British Minister of Education, as a country where education is a religion, and we are disposed to take McCarthyist assaults on intellectuals as exceptions that prove the rule. On the contrary, they are outbreaks of an enduring and smoldering suspicion of the intellectual. The cause of this suspicion is complex: the American drive toward practice, the Protestant work ethic, the glorification of business success, the influence of the frontier, religious conservatism, the association of the intellectual with effeminacy and with radicalism, and much else. Furthermore, we have had no received authorities to place laurels on appropriate brows; it is painful to think how a writer like Melville or a scientist like Josiah Willard Gibbs could live and die among us almost unrecognized. Too often in a democracy the jury that determines distinction is the longest queue at the box office. If Rita Hayworth were speaking today on any campus in the country, I suppose the hall would be full; if Emily Greene Balch were announced, the general response would be, "Who in the world is she?" She was in fact one of three American women to win the Nobel prize. Democracy and distinction are often neighbors, but one of them has a way of passing the other in the street without noticing him.

We lack the help in discerning distinction that older societies are likely to have. We have no institutions that carry the weight of Oxford and Cambridge in England, no French Academy to tap "immortals" for membership, little or none of that reverence for the Herr Professor that is part of the German tradition. Candidates for popular suffrage have been warned against looking and sounding like intellectuals ever since Andrew Jackson, described as "the unlettered man of the West, the nursling of the wild . . . little versed in books," slaughtered at the polls John Quincy Adams, President of the American Academy of Arts and Sciences and a product of Harvard, Paris, Amsterdam, and The Hague. The record even of the presidency in the nineteenth century is so lacking in intellectual distinction that James Bryce in *The American Commonwealth* has a chapter entitled "Why Great Men Are Not Chosen Presidents." Of course they don't always lose; I doubt if Bryce would have used that title after Wilson; and the American people rather took Adlai Stevenson to their hearts for losing so gaily with his hopeless appeal, "eggheads of the world, unite; you have nothing to lose but your yolks."

I have been defending this breed of eggheads to which, like some other rare species, the American ecology is not especially hospitable. I have said that the university is the true preserve of this species and should devote itself to encouraging, nursing, and improving the breed. Does this mean that the many other species of *homo sapiens* should be neglected? No, not at all. To say that their place is not the university and that their admission would swamp and defeat it is not to say that their education should not be provided for. We clearly need a greater number and diversity of schools in which boys and girls whose minds are not made for the academic curriculum can find what they *are* made for and achieve their own expertise. There is not just one way of being a happy, fulfilled, and useful citizen; there are a thousand ways; and as James Anthony Froude said, "It is better that a boy should learn to make a shoe excellently than to write bad exercises in half a dozen languages." Perhaps the chief problem for educational administrators in the decades ahead is to think out the ways in which the majority of our youth whose gifts and tastes are not academic can be prepared for their own thousandfold walks in life.

But their needs are not our theme today. Our theme has been the problem suggested by the words of John W. Gardner: "The 'two souls' in the heart of every American are the devotion to equalitarianism and the attachment to individual achievement." The trouble is that the two souls tend to repel each other, democracy leveling distinction and distinction defying equality. I have argued that we cannot afford to abandon either. I have held that we must extend, if we can, that equality of consideration which gives every one his chance in the hope, to use Jefferson's blunt words, that "geniuses will be raked from the rubbish." On the other hand, when talent appears, we must recognize that it has special and stronger claims on us in virtue of what it can do for the community. Higher education must be reserved for those of unusual powers, and those alone, since to extend it to the rest is to destroy it. When we find youths with such powers, we should cherish and nourish them and carry them as far up the educational trellis as they will go, for they are our chief treasure in this all but unmanageable world. "In the conditions of modern life," said Whitehead, "the rule is absolute, the race which does not value trained intelligence is doomed." Or to put it in William James's more positive way: "The world is . . . only beginning to see that the wealth of a nation consists more than in anything else in the number of superior men that it harbors." The business of the university, as the trustee of the community, is to see that such wealth is invested early and is given back, in accordance with the best banking stewardship, not only with capital intact but with interest compounded daily.

John W. Gardner

The Individual
and Society

It may be that we have expected
too much of our universities, but I'm inclined to believe that such
expectations are a mark of faith and respect. We expect much of the
universities in terms of everyday, more or less conventional productivity — teaching large numbers, advancing knowledge, serving the
community. In quite prosaic terms, we expect them to carry heavy
burdens in the heat of the day.

But we expect more than this. We believe that out of those
extraordinary institutions will come the deeper insights and under-
standings that will keep our civilization alive and keep it humane.

I want to discuss here one of the most perplexing problems facing
our society, indeed all advanced societies, today — a problem that
the universities are well equipped to deal with. The problem, stated
as briefly as possible, is that it has become increasingly difficult for
modern man to balance the claims of individuality and the claims of
community. No institution in our national life is better fitted than the
university to understand all that is at stake in maintaining that
balance.

We seek a society that has at its core a respect for the dignity and worth of the individual, a society that pursues fulfillment and growth for the individual. But we recognize that the deepest threat to the integrity of any community is an incapacity on the part of the citizens to lend themselves to any worthy common purpose, and we see the barrenness of a life that encompasses nothing beyond the self. As Tillich put it, the individual must have the courage to be himself and the courage to be part of something larger.

Gone forever is the unplanned, tradition-dictated submergence of the individual in the community that has existed throughout most of human history. But the balance we seek today is threatened from two sides. At one extreme, not only totalitarianism but some of the modes of large-scale organization present in our own society threaten to smother every trace of individuality. At the other extreme we see varieties of individualism that are destructive of community.

All complex modern societies, whatever their ideology, appear to be moving toward the beehive model. The intricate and precisely orchestrated organizational patterns that come so naturally to advanced technological societies are sooner or later destructive of individuality — unless extraordinary efforts are made to prevent that outcome. The trend is as evident in our own society as it is in explicitly totalitarian societies, although it is less advanced with us and is often retarded by our political guarantees of individual freedom.

The aims and consequences of political totalitarianism are well understood. Less well understood are the consequences of some of our own forms of large-scale organization, which have a clear tendency to dwarf the individual even though their purposes and methods may be authentically nontotalitarian in origin.

This is a crucial point because in our society today the individual moves in a world characterized by ever larger and more elaborately interlocking organization. It is not just that gigantic organizations — corporate, union, governmental — impinge upon the individual's life at every point. It is that the nation — and increasingly the world — has itself become one huge interlocking system. The actions of government have large consequences in the corporate and union world; actions by farm groups affect what housewives pay for groceries; the market strategies of foreign oil producers affect the American commuter; and the monetary decisions of the United States affect every nation in the world.

The advantages of large-scale organization are obvious. It brings us consumer goods, from automobiles to hi-fi sets, that would never have come out of cottage industry. It brings us kidney dialysis machines, "Sesame Street," cheap long-distance calls, efficient air transport. Some critics say they could live without those things, but very few do.

But no contemporary needs to be told of the disadvantages of large-scale organization. Too often it induces a sense of powerlessness, a loss of identity, and a feeling of anonymity. Too often it depersonalizes human relationships, erodes human communication, suppresses individuality. In subtle and not-so-subtle ways it induces conformity. The individual tends to be coerced by the system — and frustrated in ways that have a special capacity to baffle and madden.

These layered frustrations have produced a hostility and distrust that is directed at virtually all aspects of modern organized society. This hostility is directed against bureaucracy, hierarchy, administrators, monolithic institutions. In its more extreme manifestations, it is even directed against the rationality and functional efficiency that are essential to modern organization.

Multiple frustrations are not new to mankind. From the dawn of time man has been frustrated by forces and circumstances beyond his understanding. But apparently it is easier — or seems easier — to accept blows from an inscrutable fate, from natural forces or from the hand of God than to have one's life disrupted by an unknown bureaucrat presiding over an unseen computer. The hostility directed toward the administrator in an administered age is something to contend with. It has led to a kind of inarticulate rebellion that seethes in the breast of even the most conventional individual.

But indiscriminate hostility toward institutions won't help. We have to take the steps that will save us. We cannot do without large-scale organization — but we can demand that it be so designed as to serve humane purposes, and we are just beginning to understand some of the ways in which this might be done. We are beginning to understand how we might create human-sized units within large-scale organization — in factories, in higher education, in some of the newest housing developments. We must devise residential and working arrangements that enable individuals to live their lives as whole persons, not split into fragments by the requirements of a complex, impersonal society.

We must design many varying forms of participation, so that the individual can regain the sense of acting and initiating. This will involve the redesign of huge bureaucratic units to devolve more responsibility to lower levels. It will also require that we supplement the "top down" communication characteristic of large-scale organization with two-way communication that brings messages from the lower levels of organization to the top. Such two-way communication is not only sound democratic doctrine, it is a characteristic of all healthy systemic functioning. Yet most large-scale organizations sooner or later develop a severe breakdown in communication between the "grass roots" and the top.

Politically, participation requires improved citizen access to the political process, and that is not really possible until we cure politicians of their bad habit of doing the public's business behind closed doors. From the city councils and school boards up through the state legislatures to Congress and the federal agencies, elected and appointed officials find it all too convenient to do the public's business in secret. The effect on citizen awareness and interest is devastating. The citizen can't possibly develop an intelligent interest in matters that are totally hidden from his view.

Another measure necessary for the protection of the individual is the preservation of the guarantees of individual liberty written into our Constitution. There will inevitably arise from time to time, both in the public and private sectors, leaders who imagine that a huge and complex society could be far more tidily managed if those guarantees were abrogated. It is particularly important to strengthen — greatly strengthen — the protective measures that insure individual liberty and privacy. Modern forms of organization, media of communication, computerized information systems, and surveillance techniques vastly increase the capacity of the society to invade the privacy and curtail the rights of the individual. We must devise new protections against new dangers.

Yet another vital step that applies to both public- and private-sector organizations is the necessary creation of imaginative, sophisticated, and effective devices for the redress of grievances. Such devices would be directly responsive to the sense of individual powerlessness and frustration.

But the balance between the claims of individuality and the claims of community is threatened from another direction. We have considered the dangers posed by a vast, highly organized society. We must now look at the dangers posed by anarchic individualism.

Before doing so, let us remind ourselves of what is of value in the concern that we have for the individual. A concern for the individual — which entered Western history with the Renaissance — has contributed important ingredients to the best of contemporary social thinking, among them the idea that each person is of value; that all individuals are equally worthy of our care and concern; that the dignity and worth of the individual is not to be measured in terms of race, sex, status, or achievement; that society benefits in vitality as

well as stability if there is wide opportunity for individual initiative
and responsibility.

At every stage these ideas have had to be defended bitterly against
old-style tyranny; against the constraints upon the individual intrinsic
to highly stratified traditional societies; and more recently against the
all-too-successful thrust of modern totalitarian ideas. Those who have
defended the individual in those battles want no retreat.

Unfortunately the idea of individualism has also been used to
justify extremes of self-aggrandizing and antisocial behavior, whether
the wanton destruction of the environment by an unconcerned indus-
trialist or the buying and selling of hard drugs by a young person who
scorns the laws of the community. From this point of view, individualism means that when my purposes and the purposes of the society
collide, my purposes are of course paramount. A century from now
social historians will look back with astonishment at the extremes of
atomistic individualism that were celebrated in late twentieth-century
literature and social philosophy. And then the historians may have
formulated an hypothesis to explain the fact that these excesses of
individualism seemed to grow more lurid at precisely the time when
the very idea of individuality was under threat by modern technology
and large-scale social organization.

All our knowledge of human functioning, ancient or modern,
primitive or civilized, tells us that unqualified individualism is an
impossibility, an absurdity, a fantasy. By the time one is old enough
to have any kind of independence, one is inescapably a social being.
Total individualism isn't an option.

The individual can move toward the freedom available to humans
only when he recognizes that he is not wholly free. He lives with the
biological potentialities and limitations of a species that has not really
changed significantly in fifty thousand years. He lives in a cultural
context, some of which has roots that run back ten thousand years.
He is part of history, caught in the play of social forces.

When he understands that, whether the terms of his understanding are religious or philosophical, when he admits that he is part of something larger, then the only freedom that is possible to man opens up to him. Freedom is not the fulfillment of whim. Nor is it the fantasy of personal control over events and nature and others and oneself.

Recognition of one's part in a larger drama may lead to various forms of retreat and passivity. But many wise and deep humans have continued to play their role to the hilt, knowing that they are not the authors of the great drama in which they act, but acting nonetheless, with courage and a sense of purpose.

One natural corrective both to anarchic individualism and to the hazards of mass society is a healthy sense of community — but communities are vanishing from the scene. It is increasingly hard to find coherent social contexts within which individuals can find membership, or to which they can give allegiance. For too many people there is no community that they can accept as defining, in part, who they are or what their values and obligations are. The extended family is virtually extinct, and communities in the geographical sense are disintegrating. The sense of membership and allegiance stemming from a common religion or class or economic background is fading. In short, practically every kind of human community is disappearing, and those that remain exercise little command over the loyalties, imagination or daily behavior of their members.

It is a curious fact that liberals and conservatives collaborated to produce the breakdown of community. Liberals, chafing under the old order, developed emancipated ways of thinking that contributed to the passing of traditional communities. But industrialists, particularly in the fields of transportation and communication — industrialists who thought of themselves as conservatives — probably did more to disintegrate the old-style communities than all the liberals who ever lived.

What can we do about it? If we make no effort we are, in effect, deciding to let the forms and patterns of human interaction be determined by the impersonal dynamics of large-scale organization, by the unintended consequences of technological advance, and by commercially motivated decisions.

First, we can face up to the fact that no society can wholly reject its past. Justice Holmes said, "Continuity with the past is not a duty, only a necessity." A discriminating regard for the past will lead us to think twice before destroying existing communities. At the very least, we can stop standing by passively while technological advances, large-scale organization, and random commercial forces destroy elements of community that we would wish to preserve. And we can discredit the extreme individualism that has wreaked such havoc on the whole concept of community.

But holding on to the best of what remains of traditional communities isn't enough. We must experiment with new forms of community, building necessary continuities into the new forms and letting the new wholes develop organically. To enable the individual to enjoy a sense of community, a sense of belonging, we must recreate communities within the massive agglomerations of humanity that characterize contemporary life, communities that will be wholly compatible with the concept of individual worth, dignity, and creativity. Within those communities, individuals must have not only the opportunity to participate, to have their say, they must have opportunities to serve, to be needed, to "connect."

In asserting the value of "community" one need not assume that we ever can or will have a tightly knit society. The United States has never had a tightly woven social fabric and probably never will. Compared with the web of European culture from which the American colonists emerged, the new American communities were loose and pluralistic. And from our beginnings, we've moved so fast and changed so swiftly that a highly coherent culture has never emerged.

It would be wrong, of course, to imagine that giving thought to social arrangements will solve all the problems of the individual and society. Quite aside from social arrangements, the individual must come to terms with himself or herself, which isn't easy today. Old communities and belief systems have broken down. With few exceptions a swiftly changing society has withdrawn from the individual the emotional supports of custom, tradition, family solidarity, religion, stable relationships, codes of conduct, and community coherence. The individual is acutely aware of the limits on his capacity to shape events and their consequences.

At the same time the disintegration of old contexts for the self has created the new problem of "identity." In a day when families and traditions were stable, when national and local loyalties were powerful, young people didn't ask "Who am I?" They knew. They knew where they belonged, what they believed, whom they were loyal to and what was expected of them. They were defined by family, social class, ethnic tradition, economic status, parental occupation, religion.

To be sure, there were those who deviated from what was expected of them, but even their rebellion was an expression of identity. They knew precisely what they were rebelling against.

It isn't that easy today. Part of the problem lies in a wrongheaded contemporary notion of what constitutes identity. If the young person has any marks of lineage, regional style, economic status or religious beliefs, our contemporary culture tells him to ignore them or rid himself of them. Presumably one couldn't possibly accept such "accidents" of background as one's "real identity."

So young people search desperately for an "identity" that has nothing to do with the boring realities of personal background. Not surprisingly, they often seize on the fads of the moment — clothes, slang, tastes in music, manners, and attitudes. So in the end his contemporaries — or the commercial interests that invent and exploit the fads of his contemporaries — determine what the young person

comes to think of as his or her identity. Young people searching for
an identity among the popular fads and postures of the moment are
bound to believe that those exhilarating mannerisms they are trying
on for size are more interesting than anything in their own history.

But the manufactured "self" is never as interesting, never as
unique as the real person hidden underneath the hastily acquired
outer image. And the real person is a product of things pushed aside
in the search for identity: family and family relationships, ethnic
background, neighborhood surroundings during childhood, religion,
and much more. All of these interact with the individual's unique
combination of physical and mental qualities. Even if people have
grown far beyond their points of origin, even if they have rebelled
against their backgrounds, they bear the marks — as individuals —
of their origins, of the paths they have traveled and of present realities.
It's all a part of the same tapestry. And some figures in the tapestry —
one's physical and cultural heritage — may reach back through
thousands of years of history.

Another obstacle in the search for identity is the difficulty many
contemporaries have in seeing that "identity" is inseparable from
commitments, obligations, involvements, loyalties. One recognizes
the charm of the contemporary fantasy of a life with "no strings."
But identity flows in part from one's courage to commit oneself —
to enduring relationships, to the service of chosen values, to membership in a community, to a way of life.

Among other things, adult commitments help in one of the
great tasks of mental health: escaping the prison of the self. Self-
preoccupation is not without its attractions. Selfishness pays dividends; self-indulgence has multiple rewards; self-pity is deeply satisfying; even self-castigation can yield pleasure. But they are toxic
joys. Self-absorption is a prison. And that is something that every
self-absorbed person finally knows.

The escape from the prison of the self may be through religion, through dedication to a social purpose, through loving relations with other human beings. Contempt for others, paranoia, exclusion and rejection of others are all paths to self-isolation. Love breaks down the walls of the isolated self.

And crucial to constructive relations with others is a healthy self-regard. If you don't like yourself, it is difficult to maintain loving relations with others. Self-contempt is a profoundly destructive emotion — destructive to the self and to others. Perhaps the only more destructive emotion is the pleasurable but deadly poison of self-pity.

Another step in coming to terms with one's self is the achievement of some measure of self-command. One encounters in contemporary thinking a variety of arguments — some of them valid — favoring self-indulgence, unlimited self-expression, and immediate impulse gratification. But the postponement of immediate gratification, the discipline of impulse, in the interest of later rewards is at the heart of civilized life. All the great civilizations in their periods of rising vitality have cultivated a measure of austerity, of self-discipline.

But the most crucial means of coming to terms with the self is yet to be mentioned. Our polity is built on the idea of individual moral responsibility, and the polity will only survive if the idea survives. It has been eroded by many features of the contemporary scene: the sheer size and complexity of our society, which diminishes the individual's sense of involvement; the reigning environmentalism which lets the individual off the hook ("Society's to blame; I have nothing to do with it"); the almost universal habit of self-exoneration and self-deception which eliminates the possibility of individual moral responsibility by preventing the issue from being posed.

A more subtle escape from individual responsibility is described by Rollo May. He points out that by denying our power many never face the moral and ethical issue of how we use our power. Expressions of helplessness become a way of evading responsibility — "What can

I do?" May suggests a new "ethic of intention," which would assert that each individual is responsible for the effects of his or her actions.

There is much to be said for his view. Complete determinism deadens the impulse toward self-improvement, the sense of responsibility, and the moral impulse. Human choice is limited, but it is thus all the more crucial that we exercise what choice we have.

All of these considerations are ones which the university can help us to understand and live with. More than most human institutions, the university is committed to the idea of individual worth and dignity. Yet the university is a profoundly social venture, deeply and inextricably linked to its particular cultural tradition. Though it often plays an adversary role with respect to the powers and principalities, it is an indispensable bearer of the society's tradition. It is almost, one might say, the society's memory.

No other institution can better comprehend the complex issues and values at stake in the balance between the claims of individuality and the claims of community. Not only because of the knowledge it commands but because of the kind of community it is and the values it cherishes, the university is well equipped to understand and clarify the dilemmas involved in that precarious balance. It can remind us that our dilemmas have a long history. It can make us know the rich resource and burden that is our own past. It can deepen our knowledge of ourselves and the world around us. It can sharpen our sensitivities and make us aware of conflict and choice in values. It can force us to clarify the standards we set for ourselves. It can call us to the best in our own tradition.

In our present perplexity, those are not negligible contributions.

T. R. McConnell

Surfeit or Dearth of Highly Educated People?

The movement from elite to mass, and in the United States to something approaching universal higher education, has significantly changed the labor market for college-trained men and women. The British have become particularly sensitive to this transition as they look forward to what is for them a great expansion of full-time and part-time higher education. Graduation from the elite sector of British higher education — the universities — has in the past been the avenue to high social status and to preferential positions in education, industry, government, and the professions. But a former president of the British Association of University Teachers recently warned that, "As we move from an elite to a mass system of higher education, it is more than obvious that a degree which is open to up to 25 percent of the age group can no longer be an exclusive passport to the top five percent of the jobs. Many jobs which were formerly done by nongraduates will have to be done by graduates." [1]

---

[1] H. J. Perkin, "President's Opening Address to Council," *A. U. T. Bulletin* 39 (London, June 1971): 18.

The Confederation of British Industry has predicted that the number of jobs industry considers appropriate for graduates will not increase as fast as the supply of graduates in the next ten years, and that if a greater output is to be absorbed, many graduates will have to look to a wider range of jobs and an increased acceptance of positions below the traditional level.[2] Appointment to government positions is a case in point. In 1970 the British Civil Service recruited seven hundred graduates to the executive class, for which a degree had not normally been required, and only about one hundred to the administrative class, the traditional degree-level division. Even graduates in science, engineering, and technology have been forced to consider a much greater variety of openings than they did even two or three years ago. The British concept of the "graduate job" is steadily waning and may completely disappear.[3]

The United States is already experiencing acutely what the British are anticipating, experience which may be partially responsible for the slowing down in postsecondary enrollment. Although the Carnegie Commission on Higher Education has estimated that in the United States two-thirds of the eighteen- to twenty-one-year-old group will enter some form of postsecondary schooling within the foreseeable future, the enormous increase in college enrollment which occurred in the last two decades cannot be sustained. With evidence at hand that 637,000 fewer students were enrolled in 1973 than previously estimated, and that the shortfall would be 578,000 in 1974, the Carnegie Commission reduced its prediction of total enrollment in the 1980's from 13,015,000 to 11,446,000; from 12,654,000 to 10,555,000 in 1990; and from 16,559,000 to 13,209,000 in 2000. It reduced its projection of a 51 percent increase in enrollment during

---

[2] *Times Higher Education* Supplement (London), 28 January 1972.

[3] See Harriet Greenaway, "The Impact of Educational Policies," in Harriet Greenaway and Gareth Williams, *Patterns of Change in Graduate Employment* (London: Society for Research into Higher Education, 1973), pp. 1–23.

the decade 1970–80 to 33 percent. Dr. Lyman Glenny, director of the Center for Research and Development in Higher Education in the University of California at Berkeley, considers the Carnegie Commission's revised predictions to be still too optimistic.[4]

In spite of a diminished rate of growth in postsecondary education, we are likely to have what some observers would consider to be a plethora of highly educated people as measured by the educational requirements of the labor force. It has been estimated that only 20 percent of jobs will require education beyond the high school. Yet 50 percent of the eighteen- to twenty-one-year age group attend college at some point. The current discrepancy between the percentage of jobs requiring some higher education and the percentage of the age group attending college for some period of time is thus 30 percent, and the estimated potential discrepancy is nearly 50 percent.[5]

What are some of the consequences of the apparent surplus of educated people? First of all, as noted above, college and university graduates will have to consider a wider range of occupations, and many of them will have to accept positions below those traditionally held by graduates; many of these positions will not make full use of the education of those who hold them. It has been pointed out that even now nearly 30 percent of male four-year college graduates are in blue-collar, sales, and clerical jobs, many of which do not make full use of their training.[6]

As they are filled by college graduates, some positions will undoubtedly be genuinely upgraded to the point where the operational requirements are of a truly higher order than when the jobs were filled by nongraduates. In a very large number of instances, however,

---

[4] Lyman A. Glenny, "The Sixties in Reverse," *Research Reporter* 8, no. 3 (1973): 1–4.

[5] Carnegie Commission on Higher Education, *College Graduates and Jobs* (New York: McGraw-Hill, 1973), pp. 2–3.

[6] Ibid., p. 4.

the educational requirements of a wide range of positions will be raised well above the actual levels of intelligence, knowledge, and skill required for acceptable performance. Consequently, it has been said, what is usually called an oversupply of educated persons might better be called a supply of overeducated persons.[7]

Another response to the scarcity of "suitable" positions is for graduates to take advanced degrees as a means of meeting competition. The United States is suffering from an oversupply of elementary, secondary, and college teachers. Holders of the baccalaureate who do not find positions in the schools are likely to stay on for a master's, and those with the master's degree who desire but fail to find positions in community colleges will go on to the doctorate. This has already led to a current surplus of Ph.D.'s. It does not follow, however, that many people with doctorates will be unemployed for any extended period. The "extra" Ph.D.'s will displace those with lower degrees in positions not previously requiring a higher credential.

The response of institutions of higher education themselves to the employment conditions sketched above are predictable. In Britain, for example, undergraduate courses for certificates or diplomas will ultimately be upgraded to programs for the first degree. Thus teaching, which has been entered by persons holding certificates rather than degrees, is to become an all-graduate profession. Postgraduate courses for diplomas will be extended to courses for advanced degrees, although this trend will be slowed somewhat by the policy of the University Grants Committee to restrict growth in postgraduate enrollment. The British universities, responding to social pressures and to competition from the thirty recently designated polytechnics, will be more hospitable to education for the newer professions. Nursing, which has had little more than a foothold in the universities, will

---

[7] See L. B. DeWitt and A. D. Tussing, *The Supply and Demand for Graduates of Higher Education: 1970–80* (Syracuse, N.Y.: Educational Policy Center, Syracuse University, 1971), p. 8.

become a recognized university subject. Britain's long tradition of apprenticeship and learning on the job will probably give way to formal college courses leading to degrees, for example, in accountancy and law. "All teachers in all schools, estate agents, foremen in factories — the list of potential upgradings is a long one." [8]

The British universities will probably continue to make a relatively conservative response to education for the newer professions, but popular institutions of mass higher education — the polytechnics, with the mandate to serve their communities, regions, and the national interest — will respond willingly, even enthusiastically, as did the land-grant colleges and state universities in the United States, to new social, economic, and cultural pressures and opportunities.

Students, who are surprisingly sensitive to changes in the job market and who can be made even more so by appropriate career and educational counseling, may be expected to shift from surplus fields to occupations where there are shortages of personnel. In the United States such fields are nursing and other allied health professions, chemistry, counseling, dietetics, social work, urban planning and local government. Furthermore, new occupations are appearing. In the field of health alone, it has been estimated that there are more than two hundred specialties associated with improvements in health care. It has been predicted that in the United States, the number of allied health specialists requiring at least a baccalaureate degree will increase from 229,500 in 1967 to 410,000 in 1980, and that those requiring less than the baccalaureate will increase from 424,000 to 656,000.

The futurists seem to agree that the "new world" will be built on amazing developments in science and technology which will require high levels of specialization but a relatively small number of specialists. British educators have been greatly concerned over a recent

---

[8] B. J. Holloway, "Careers for Graduates," *Times Educational Supplement* (London), 7 February 1971.

swing away from science. They have adjusted to this change in students' interests reluctantly. For example, they have consistently provided more places for science students in the universities than were justified by student demands, so that to the dismay of science faculties, the level of previous achievement necessary for admission to university science departments has steadily declined. Having heard widespread expressions of concern over the declining interest in science, I was astonished recently to hear a distinguished British scientist now in a position of high leadership in the university system declare that relatively fewer scientists and technologists would be needed in British industry in the future, and that the great expansion in higher education in the next decade would have to be in the social services rather than in science and engineering.

The need in the United States for the expansion and the support of human services is enormous. Such services include health, education and research, the arts, religion, and government. "These are the activities," said Howard R. Bowen, chancellor of the Claremont University Center, recently, "that touch individuals profoundly, that determine the range of their opportunity and that affect not only their welfare but also their capacity to become full-fledged human beings." Yet, he declared, these are the very activities which we are supporting penuriously. He went on to say that the human services which could be advantageously provided appear to be almost unlimited. His illustrations are worth quoting at some length:

> Suppose, for example, we were to provide at the highest professional level all the dental service that is needed for the whole population, or all the psychiatric service or all the legal help. How many dentists or psychiatrists or lawyers would be needed?
> Suppose the nation embarked on early childhood education and universal child care programs with compensatory education for the underprivileged. How many teachers would be needed?
> Suppose we were to provide art museums and symphony orchestras and theatre throughout the country as many European

countries do. How many artists, musicians and actors would be needed?

Suppose our local governments were to be adequately staffed to control crime, to improve waste disposal and water supply, to carry out proper land-use planning, to organize adequate parks and recreation, etc. How many local government officials and other workers would be needed?

Suppose our churches were to be properly manned with professional workers. How many clergymen and religious workers would be needed?

Suppose we undertook a nationwide program of continuing higher education. How many university professors would be needed?

It is not hard to conjure up ideas to employ millions of people to provide services that any reasonable person would regard as desirable.[9]

Providing these services is not a matter of technique alone, however. Speaking of the competence required, a British observer has said: "The ability to think rationally and in depth, to form judgments, to present ideas in a logical and coherent fashion and then to implement resultant decisions are qualities in as much demand in the public service as in industry or commerce." [10] These are the capabilities which higher education should engender.

Graduates will not only have to accept positions once considered inappropriate for holders of college and university degrees, but many of them will have to be content with modest incomes. A recent study of graduate employment in Britain showed that whereas in 1962 the average starting salary of science and technology graduates was about the same as the average earnings of manual workers, in 1972 the average wage of an adult manual employee was about 30 percent higher than a graduate's starting salary.[11] The Carnegie Commission

---

[9] Howard R. Bowen, quoted in the *University of Iowa Spectator* 7 (October 1973): 2.

[10] Greenaway, "Impact of Educational Policies," pp. 18–19.

[11] Gareth Williams and Harriet Greenaway, "The New Proletarians," *Times Higher Education Supplement* (London), 28 September 1973.

on Higher Education has pointed out that in the United States wage and salary differentials of graduates and nongraduates will gradually decrease. For example, academic salaries and incomes of plumbers, electricians, and some other highly skilled craftsmen have been converging. I recently facetiously asked an administrator at Berkeley how many assistant professors had asked to be transferred to the maintenance staff after the latter had secured a large pay increase. As salary differentials between graduates and nongraduates continue to decrease, the personal rate of economic return on a college education will diminish. College students' traditional repudiation of materialistic values may be severely tested.

As universal access to higher education materializes, societal economic benefit may also decline. Economists tend to evaluate the advantages of increasing the financial support for higher education in terms of social benefits, and often assume that it is appropriate for individuals to defray the cost of purely personal returns. It has proved extremely difficult, however, to estimate the personal and social benefits of different levels of education, and attempts to do so have proved to be highly unreliable. Dr. Charles Carter, economist and vice-chancellor of the University of Lancaster in Britain, who has directed cost studies in British universities and carefully examined the technique of cost–benefit analysis, has concluded that, "the social return to higher education, as usually calculated, is a useless figure." Even the manpower approach to justifying the outcomes of higher education has proved to be highly unsatisfactory, since estimates of future needs for educated personnel have proved to be highly unreliable. Where have these deficiencies left us?

Carter has declared that by ignoring the real purposes of higher education, economists have led us up blind alleys. He concedes that economists can help higher education make efficient use of the resources given to it, but insists that they "should not seek to determine the quantum of these resources, by arguments which implicitly assume that the prime purpose of society is to get richer." Declaring that the vocational purposes of higher education are incidental and secondary, Carter goes on:

> The principal reason why we have universities and colleges is concerned with the extension of civilisation, with the rediscovery of man's highest creative achievements, with the need in every generation to question and challenge what has been created, and with the excitement of new discovery. The benefit is, or should be, the enlargement of culture and the enlivening of minds. The cost is whatever, with good planning, is needed to achieve that end . . . . We have damaged the cause of civilisation and culture by trying to convince people that they are "good business," and that education has a yield as good as that of a jam factory . . . . Perhaps the greatest harm which has been done by the jam factory approach is to rob that part of education which is concerned with the summits of human achievement, and with the boundaries at which we confront our vast ignorance and inadequacy, of the awe and wonder which should surround it. It is a poor, silly thing to attach to the discovery of the imperishable beauty of great writing, of the profundity of philosophy, of the orderly subtlety of pure mathematics, a money value in increasing national production.[12]

Elsewhere Carter has said, "even if it could be shown that the economic system has no need of any extension of higher education we would all still argue in favor of providing it, for surely education should be judged by its contribution to the quality of civilisation and to the happiness and self-fulfillment of human beings. It is a poor, silly doctrine which looks at it as an ancillary in the production of material wealth." [13]

However, Carter is not talking about purely selfish returns to the individual. Unless a liberal education inculcates a heightened sense

---

[12] Charles F. Carter, "Costs and Benefits of Mass Higher Education," *Higher Education* 2 (May 1973): 206–13.

[13] Charles F. Carter, "Conclusion," in G. Brosan et al., *Patterns and Policies in Higher Education* (Harmondsworth, England: Penguin, 1971), pp. 183–86.

of social responsibility and service, and in that sense makes a fundamental contribution to the general welfare, the public may withhold support on the ground that the educational benefits are too heavily private. "The man of humane sentiments and sensibilities, the whole civilised man," writes Carter, "will be concerned with the impact of advanced technology on society, the relationships of nation states, the problems of human relationships in the family and in urban society, and the enrichment of life for everyone." [14] The social benefits of these educational values may be hard to quantify, but they nonetheless express the hopes of civilized man as well as faith in the humane values of higher education.

Postsecondary institutions will have to train workers in a great variety of fields and at different levels of complexity. The University of Utah, for example, will need to educate specialists and professionals of the highest quality and to lead other universities in meeting social needs more imaginatively and effectively, as it has, for example, in medicine. Essential as vocational preparation is, I believe that the primary purpose of colleges and universities alike is to provide the means of general and liberal education. Looking to the postindustrial society, Galbraith has said that instead of becoming captives of the industrial system, "colleges and universities can strongly assert the values and goals of educated men — those that serve not the production of goods and associated planning but the intellectual and artistic development of man." [15] Kahn and Wiener, in envisaging the year 2000, point out that the economy will be capable of producing a vast increase in goods and in such services as transportation and communication. It will also be capable of begetting a great increase in leisure with a concomitant reduction in the pressures of work. They

---

[14] Charles F. Carter, "Variety and Visions," in Brosan et al., *Patterns and Policies in Higher Education*, pp. 77–89.

[15] John Kenneth Galbraith, *The New Industrial State* (Boston: Houghton-Mifflin, 1967), p. 291.

warn that the drastically reduced work week, earlier retirement, and longer vacations could be more dangerous than benign. Leisure may encourage self-indulgence and irresponsibility. "Thus there may be a great increase in selfishness, a great decline of interest in government and society as a whole, and a rise in the more childish forms of individualism . . . ." [16]

Fortunately, there are other possibilities. Kahn and Wiener say that they can imagine "a situation in which, say, 70 percent or 80 percent of people become gentlemen and put a great deal of effort into various types of self-improvement . . . . One could imagine, for example, a very serious emphasis on sports, . . . on music, art, language, or serious travel, or on the study of science, philosophy, and so on." [17] Postindustrial man can use his free time for ever more frenetic and unrewarding pleasure, or he can turn it into a means of self-fulfillment and a better life for all men everywhere. The purpose of liberal education is to enable him to do just that.

But is it not futile to propose the revival of liberal education at the very moment students seem to be turning away from it? We are told that students are shunning liberal arts colleges to enter public institutions which offer varied occupational curricula. Even Antioch College, which has long offered a work–study program, has had difficulty in attracting its normal intake of freshmen. Many students especially interested in career education have entered proprietary and industrial schools rather than community colleges or four-year colleges and universities. Four-year public institutions are beginning to offer more nondegree curricula; community colleges are reducing the component of general education in their curricula and offering shorter intensive technical and other applied programs. Dr. Lyman Glenny wrote recently that young people, "rather than being stitched

---

16 Herman Kahn and A. J. Wiener, *The Year 2000: A Framework for Specu-lation on the Next Thirty-three Years* (New York: Macmillan Co., 1967), p. 199.
17 Ibid., p. 217.

and laced with liberal arts, are turning to institutions whose programs are more responsive to their needs." [18] I do not know what stitching and lacing students with liberal arts means, but I presume it implies that general education imprisons the student in irrelevancy and inhibits the attainment of his legitimate purposes. But I suggest that the student's goals are not always wise or the means he uses to attain them certain to be effective. I can see a need for intensive specialized courses at whatever level they may be productive. I cannot believe, however, that either technical or professional education should be pursued in narrow perspective. Again we may look to British education for illumination. Britain has an amazing network of technical and specialized institutions offering a range of courses from those for people who leave school at fifteen or sixteen all the way to courses for postgraduate diplomas and degrees. These are highly specialized institutions, although courses in the arts and social sciences are by no means entirely excluded, nor are the scientific foundations of technical and technological processes ignored. However, leaders in technical education increasingly stress the need for broader training and the impracticality of acquiring skill without reference to the setting in which it will be used. One of the most perceptive leaders in technical and technological education is Sir Peter Venables. He has served as director of the Birmingham College of Technology; director of the College of Advanced Technology, into which the former college evolved; and, finally, as vice-chancellor of the University of Aston, which succeeded the College of Advanced Technology. Speaking at a recent British–American conference on education and work, Sir Peter asserted that "Vocational determinism is out, and technical training no longer a sufficient justification for an educational institution." He insisted that the proper study of mankind is an integral part of technical, business, and management studies because the

---

[18] Glenny, "Sixties in Reverse," p. 4.

major problems of commerce and industry are no longer technologi-cal but human.[19]

Although there are many arguments for pursuing general and specialized education together, one must admit that neither in the college nor the university — nor in a lifetime — is there but one pro-ductive combination or sequence of general and specialized studies. In college it should be possible to move from general to special, or from special to general, or to pursue both kinds of studies together throughout the undergraduate years, although perhaps with chang-ing emphasis. Likewise, it should be possible — in fact it will become increasingly necessary — to engage in a comparable sequence or combination of courses throughout one's active productive and intel-lectual life.

Sir Peter referred also to the need for longer basic courses and the deferment of specialization, perhaps until after the first degree, as an alternative to the attempt to produce a complete professional or executive on graduation day. The trend toward longer and broader undergraduate education is especially significant in Britain, which has long placed a premium on relatively specialized secondary school preparation for university studies and which has exalted specialized honors courses, often in a single department or faculty, for the first degree. A broad basic education should provide the foundation for continued intellectual growth and for the changing requirements of a successful career.

However essential general education may be in principle, it has all too frequently been ineffective in practice. Clark Kerr has said that in fact general education is a disaster area. And so it has become, for many reasons. A principal one is that university and even college faculty members have been trained as specialists and as specialists

---

19 Peter Venables, "Dissolving the Walls Between the Worlds of Education and Work" (Paper prepared for an Anglo-American Conference at Ditchley Park, England, September 1973).

who more often than not, I suspect, ignore the bearings of their disciplines on other fields of study, and especially on man's understanding of himself and his social and natural environments. Furthermore, in evaluating their colleagues faculties usually reward contributions to specialized scholarship and ignore contributions to general understanding. In research universities especially, a young faculty member can easily sacrifice departmental advancement by spending the time which the imaginative development of interdisciplinary courses requires. A man without a department is even more vulnerable. A new Berkeley faculty member is just such a man without a country. Responsible to an energy resources committee, the new staff member, presumably believing that the energy problem cannot be divorced from the social environment, either as a public issue or as a subject of academic study and investigation, will play a leading part in the development of interdisciplinary courses and seminars on energy resources and their utilization. From past experience one can predict that unless the appropriate administrative officer gives him active support, the man without a department will become a man without normal rewards for academic service. (Fortunately, the man in question has recently been promoted to higher rank.)

Perhaps the most important reason for the failure of programs of general education is sheer lack of academic and educational imagination. Or the deficiencies may be the product of sheer pedantry. For example, scholars have become highly skillful in taking the humanities to pieces and categorizing the bits without reintegrating the shattered fragments into new patterns.[20] The product is a cursory curriculum with little unity or coherence and usually with little reference to humanity. Early efforts to make general education more

---

[20] See W. R. Niblett, "Keeping the Humanities Human," in A. S. Nash, ed., *The Choice Before the Humanities* (Durham, N.C.: Regional Education Laboratory for the Carolinas and Virginia, 1970), pp. 39–55, and M. B. Smith, "Three Dirty Words: Some Thoughts on Semantics and Higher Education," pp. 23–35 in the same work.

coherent than a collection of essentially unrelated departmental offerings produced the survey course, in which, as one of my former colleagues put it, the pieces were put together on the "beads-on-a-string" scheme. More meaningful courses were organized around ideas or even more effectively around questions that would lead the student to search for ideas and their interrelationships. The purpose of one such interdisciplinary course in the humanities was "to reveal the career during the last two centuries of the idea of modern man considered as a self-governing member of self-governing communities." The course's basic content was a selection of documents primarily from history, social criticism, literature, art, and philosophy which in appropriate combination and sequence would mark the course of man's efforts to govern himself by highlighting the wide-reaching and deep-going changes in man's conception of himself, his relation to his fellow-men, and his methods of regulating human affairs. The student was encouraged to define his own role in man's restless search for self-realization, individual freedom, and social responsibility. Literature and the arts exemplify the intimate relationship of the intellect and the emotions. The course in the humanities I have been discussing was a course in ideas, but it was also a course in human experience with all the depth of feeling that that experience entails.

The humanities are not the only province of pedants. Sir Frederick Dainton, who recently left a professorship in chemistry at Oxford to become chairman of Britain's University Grants Committee, has charged that university science teachers have offered students little more than "the store of abstract theory or dull traditional experiment" rather than showing them how science could enrich their lives and how it is relevant to social issues. Scientists and other scholars cannot communicate with one another, according to Sir Frederick. Until they and the educated public can carry on a dialogue on the power and limitations of science, "Nations will fall prey to ideologies and their prophets who offer nought but an act of belief and a flight from reason." [21]

In his first address to the faculty of the University of Utah, President David Gardner, most appropriately it seems to me, emphasized the intellectual function and character of a university. "We want compassion and humanity in our students and in ourselves," he said, "but no supply of it from us toward them or from them toward themselves or us will take the place of knowledge — anymore than that knowledge, once mastered, can save us without wisdom and compassion in the use of it." [22] Recently the Honorable John Vasconcellos, chairman of the Joint Committee on Higher Education of the California legislature, in a personal letter commenting on an address I had made concerning the primacy of the university's intellectual function, suggested that the capacity for discerning right and wrong was to be found in the emotions rather than in the intellect. His attitude is indicative of the retreat from reason, the escape into feelings, and the reliance on immediate experience that mark the anti-intellectualism of our day. But it is dangerous to take experience as it comes without reflecting upon it to give it meaning, without winnowing and sifting it to find what is fundamental and lasting rather than marginal and ephemeral, without culling and screening it again and again in order to establish our directions. Education in a free society neither enthrones cold reason nor relies on emotional impulse devoid of rational choice and design. The problem we face is to subject emotion to reason and to couple intellectual solutions with feeling and commitment. Reconciling intellect and emotion, reason and feeling, is one of the principal means by which an individual determines his identity and locates himself in relation to other persons, to a wide

---

[21] *Times Higher Education Supplement* (London), 26 October 1973.

[22] David P. Gardner, "Some Reflections of a New University President" (Address delivered at the annual Faculty Breakfast, University of Utah, Salt Lake City, September 18, 1973), p. 15.

variety of groups, and to the major social issues of his time. These are means by which the individual may attain a high degree of personal autonomy and a full measure of individuality.

Learning, it is true, may be sterile if it is completely divorced from experience. There are manifold ways in which the classroom and the environment can enrich each other. To project the significance of learning for life is one means of evaluating and validating intellectual inquiry. Furthermore, experience may give impetus to systematic scholarship and to intellectual imagination. It is unexamined experience that is likely to pay poor educational dividends. One of the university's intellectual purposes, writes Lord Ashby, Master of Clare College, Cambridge, is to carry experience "from the uncritical acceptance of orthodoxy to creative dissent over the values and standards of society." [23]

Intellectual education need not, yes must not, abjure the problem of values. All of us are frequently unaware of the values which implicitly shape not only our attitudes but also our ideas. One of the principal purposes of education is to encourage the student to identify the values which guide his behavior, whether he is conscious of them or not, to subject these values to critical appraisal, and to revise them in the light of their intellectual validity and their individual and social consequences. Likewise, intellectual analysis should enable students to detect the values which are embedded in social institutions and human relationships. The crises of the moment in our national life are not really in such problems as energy and ecology, complicated and important as they are. Our gravest crises are in confidence, decency, and morality. The purpose of higher education, Lord Ashby concludes, is to "help people to learn the art of that sort of decision making which includes scientific data, estimates of practicality, and a framework of ethical principles." [24]

---

[23] Eric Ashby, "The Structure of Higher Education: A World View," *Higher Education* 2 (May 1973): 142–51.

[24] Ibid.

I remember my first visit to Utah. I was amazed at the way in which you had made the desert bloom, and I have since learned how successfully you have used science and technology in expanding your economic wealth. But I have been even more impressed with your efforts to improve the quality of life by giving your youth the opportunity for and the means of personal development and by emphasizing the highest standards of human association. This state has set an example for all the others by putting a premium on the extension of civilization, the encouragement of man's highest creative achievements, and the enlivening of the minds of the entire community. To these ends your people have supported education generously and in so doing have created a great university. I cannot imagine that the citizens of Utah will ever deal with this university penuriously, restrict educational opportunity, or compute the benefits of higher education solely in economic return to the society. On the contrary, I should expect them to agree with Lord Ashby that cost–benefit analysis applied to liberal education is a nonsense.

Mina Rees

The Ivory Tower
and the Marketplace

The decision to use the occasion of the inauguration of a distinguished new president at this university to mount an extended discussion of the meaning of the university in America at the end of the twentieth century seems to me to be a happy augury for the future. For the universities of the United States are now moving into the third major period of their lives, consummating a trend that began in colonial days. Then the colleges of the East were, to a substantial degree, a realization of the university described in 1852 by John Henry Cardinal Newman when he wrote that the university is "the high protecting power of all knowledge and science, of fact and principle, of inquiry and discovery, of experiment and speculation; it maps out the territory of the intellect, and sees that . . . there is neither encroachment nor surrender on any side." [1] He favored liberal knowledge and said that useful knowledge was "a deal of trash." To make clear what he meant by "liberal" he quoted from

---

[1] John Henry Cardinal Newman, *The Idea of a University* (Garden City, N.Y.: Image Books, 1959), p. 135.

Aristotle: "Of possessions, those . . . are useful which bear fruit; those liberal, which tend to enjoyment. By fruitful, I mean, which yield revenue; by enjoyable, where nothing accrues of consequence beyond the using."

In the early days of America, the colonial colleges, dedicated as they were not so much to preparation for a vocation as to the refinement of gentlemanly qualities, included in their student bodies primarily the most privileged young men in American society. They provided four years of maturation and leisurely acquisition of poise and knowledge in a pleasant environment. They were, in essential ways, like the ivory tower, christened by Sainte-Beuve in the nineteenth century — withdrawn from the world, encouraging an attitude of aloofness, like Thomas Carlyle's tower study in Chelsea in London, which can be reached only by a very narrow staircase; upon ascending it his friend Will Devons, lost in admiration, said, "Why, you could write up here for years and the world would never be one whit the wiser." For many years the eastern colleges did indeed work away at their own jobs, and the world was not very much the wiser. These were the colleges many of which transformed themselves in the course of their development from undergraduate colleges into major research universities. These were the colleges which, with the society they served, produced an amazing collection of Americans who made the birth of a new nation possible and who delineated hopes and purposes for that nation based on the conceptions of some of the world's greatest writers and philosophers. Today we are still grateful, as we recover from the almost unbelievable disasters that have recently befallen our corporate state, for the formulations they left us of our national identity and purpose.

The universities in England on which early American colleges were modeled were truly sanctuaries for the transmission of learning. Indeed, in the first half of *this* century, an eminent Cambridge mathematician boasted that his work would never be used. No boast was ever more futile, for mathematical results, however abstract (and including his) have a way of providing useful insights and deep understanding that can be and are used in the real world. But, whatever the usefulness of the results, many of our most powerful scholars and scientists still carry on their studies solely from a desire to understand. To provide the opportunity for such studies is a precious function of the university that it must continue to protect. It is interesting to note, however, that in recent years a number of Nobel prizes awarded for an increased understanding of the nature of matter have been awarded to scientists engaged in research in industrial laboratories. Indeed, it is characteristic of our time that much of the deepest understanding of nature and of man is being translated into use with great speed, and that the industrial users of these translations have built their own industrial research towers to encourage within their own establishments greater interplay between research and its applications. Nonetheless, I would hold that a continuing major function of the university in the United States is to support and strengthen the kind of inquiry into nature which can be pursued chiefly from a motivation to understand the world and the people in it. As Lord Eric Ashby has said, "provided students have leisure to do their own thing, the university should insist on doing *its* own thing, which is the pursuit of knowledge through rational enquiry and discourse." [2] Recently the International Council on the Future of the University formulated it this way: "The primary purpose of the University," they said, "is to transmit intellectual disciplines and seek the truth." [3]

Though I subscribe to these statements as a formulation of *one* of the major functions of the university, it is important to recognize that in this vast and varied country of ours there are many functions to be served and diverse clienteles to be educated, and it would serve us ill

---

[2] Eric Ashby, *Any Person, Any Study: An Essay on Higher Education in the United States* (New York: McGraw-Hill, 1971), p. 61.

[3] *New York Times*, 18 October 1973.

if all our universities set for themselves the same purposes, the same organizational patterns, and the same campus ambience. A recent article by Edward L. Pattulo in the *Harvard Bulletin* makes the point in an interesting way:

> My main thesis is that the complexity of higher education in the second half of the twentieth century is such that its several objectives can continue to be met only if some institutions begin to specialize. In a simpler time, a university of moderate size and good resources could serve both scholarship and the general need of undergraduates equally well. Now that education beyond the high school has become a mass phenomenon, the task of providing appropriate learning experiences for undergraduates has become immensely more complex, and involves only partially the skills and knowledge that are the special province of the scholar. It demands a large complement of teachers with interests and aptitudes specifically suited to it. At the same time, the basic fields of learning have become ever more specialized, and the role of the scholar has expanded to include many important responsibilities extending beyond the university. This combination of changes has moved research scholars and much of the undergraduate population in quite different directions; a relationship which was seldom symbiotic, but was long complementary and fruitful for both partners, has become increasingly disjunctive and deleterious.
>
> Those who understand and empathize with the needs of the majority of undergraduates can only feel enormous frustration at the glacial pace of change in most colleges and universities. Where the institution's basic *raison d'être* is the instruction and socialization of a cross-section of the young, it is reasonable and appropriate to press responsible faculties by all available means to better performance of their first duty. At Harvard, I believe the reluctance of the Faculty to embrace some of the reforms which seem so obviously needed from this perspective, stems not from recalcitrance, blindness or unconcern, but from a strong sense, hitherto unarticulated, that our most important responsibility lies elsewhere, and the changes which would be consistent with the one objective are quite inconsistent with our primary obligation to perpetuate a great scholarly community. Few can doubt that changes are needed here also, but it is likely that they are of a quite different kind than those which must take place in the

colleges and universities whose basic task is undergraduate instruction.[4]

An equally interesting statement made by the president of the University of Chicago when he addressed the incoming students in the autumn of 1971 is also worth considering:

> The original idea of this University is instructive . . . . [It] was not founded as a college, which then grew into a university . . . . [It] started both as an undergraduate college and as a major center for graduate and professional study. It placed its emphasis both on the liberal arts and upon the overwhelming importance of investigation. . . . [F]rom the very beginning . . . [t]he University . . . has attempted to make pervasive throughout the entire institution, and at all stages, its dual emphasis on the liberal arts and on investigation. . . . In short, it has never accepted the dichotomy which is supposed to separate teaching from research. It believes that discovery, itself, is the greatest form of teaching, and that mutual efforts to understand . . . not only give the institution its unity, but link scholars over time and across national boundaries and disciplines.[5]

The specializations of a university's functions represented by the reality at Chicago and by Mr. Pattulo's proposal for discussion at Harvard are two manifestations of a university's function in which the role of the ivory tower and the search for understanding are truly central. Other universities will have other central commitments, and diversity in providing for the diverse needs that higher education must serve is clearly necessary. An unfortunate concomitant of the vast expansion of higher education in the sixties was the accompanying tendency for a truly disastrous homogenization of program and purpose. Thus, when I address myself to the topic "The Meaning of the University," I shall mean the total undertaking of the system of uni-

---

[4] Edward L. Pattulo, "The Case for a Different Kind of Harvard," *Harvard Bulletin* (December 1972), p. 26.

[5] Edward H. Levi, "An Adventure in Discovery" (The University of Chicago, 1971).

versities, and shall not assume that every university should be a carbon copy of any one of them.

However much we may be committed to the value and purpose of the ivory tower in a university, we must recognize that for about a century during the second period of their growth our universities have been moving on an inexorable course toward a greater service to society and the marketplace. Since the end of the nineteenth century, when the elective system revolutionized the curricula in many of the leading colleges of the East and made possible a broadly based liberal education and scientific, professional, or scholarly training, the size of this commitment toward the marketplace has increased while its meaning has been redefined. Now, as the university in America enters the third major period in its life, like universities in many other nations of the world, it is a prime instrument of national purpose; and the scope of American society's expectations of the university has assumed troubling proportions. How did this come about?

With the daring new conception introduced by the Morrill Act of 1862, the land-grant colleges were established to provide educational support for agriculture and the mechanic arts. The act establishing these colleges set forth their leading purpose: "to teach such branches of learning as are related to agriculture and the mechanic arts . . . in order to promote the liberal and practical education of the industrial classes in the several pursuits and professions in life." [6]

As these colleges took on responsibility for the agricultural experiment stations in 1887 and the agricultural extension service in 1914, they were launched into a period of service to the American marketplace which was a forerunner of much that would come to characterize higher education in America. At virtually the same time, the concept that the university should provide a home for research and

---

[6] In H. C. Knoblauch, E. M. Law, and W. P. Meyer, *State Agricultural Experiment Stations: A History of Research Policy and Procedure* (Washington, D.C.: U.S. Government Printing Office, 1962), p. 218.

graduate education was imported from Germany. From that time onward, the genius of Americans for combining advances in knowledge with advances in its use blossomed and made possible much of this country's technological leadership.

This trend was greatly reinforced during World War II, when the federal government adapted the concept of the procurement contract, routinely used for goods and equipment, to embrace the purchase from the universities of research and development in support of military needs. The strengthening of research and development in the sciences and engineering on university campuses that was a concomitant of this decision made inevitable the post-war decision to look to the universities rather than toward independent research institutes (such as exist in some other countries) for the expansion of basic research in the sciences which was viewed as a national requirement if the country was to maintain itself in the competition for military security and industrial progress.

Initially under the sponsorship of the Office of Naval Research, and later under a score of other federal agencies, research in the sciences and, to a lesser degree, in the social sciences flourished on campuses across the land, usually in close relation to the agencies' problems. This made possible an easy flow back and forth between basic research and applications and gave the researcher the excitement that comes from seeing his often abstract results translated into significant use.

Under the stimulation of a quarter of a century of increasingly generous federal support, the United States attained a dominant position in scientific research and in the development of a science-based technology that was the envy of the world. Although the support of scientific research as well as the support of many other programs at universities has fallen on evil days with a reassessment of national priorities, a significant attitude developed during the vast expansion of federally supported campus research and graduate education has persisted to greater or lesser degree at all universities. This attitude accepts as part of the function of the university the requirement that it look outward toward the uses of the results obtained on campus and toward providing the people who can put these results (as well as their personal general sophistication in the field) to use. Faculty people on leave, students who will make their careers in business, industry, and government — basing their work on the specifics rather than the generality of their university experience — have become the shapers of important new procedures in the industrial and business world and important new products on the basis of which our increasingly sophisticated economy has developed.

Thus, in many instances, the university's responsiveness to the world about it has tended to give scope and depth to its scholarly activities.

With the coming of the 1970's with their new social values and expectations, important new forces have been felt by the universities. Always in America we have had a substantial number of students on our campuses who didn't want to be there, a number variously estimated as between 5 and 15 percent. Over the years the reasons have varied. (In March 1975 in Phoenix, Arizona, an eighteen-year-old high school senior, found guilty of an eighty-five-dollar liquor store robbery, was sentenced to two years in college as part of the terms of his five-year probation.) Now, even though over half of the age group are entering some form of postsecondary education, a significant number of our young people do not want to go to college, sometimes because the economic advantages of a college degree are proving increasingly illusory, sometimes because they do not want to be prepared for roles in a society whose values they do not respect. Many of our young people and many of us who can no longer claim to be young are disenchanted with what our society can offer us. Corruption in high office, fraud in the marketplace, political scandal accepted as normal, all these and the social injustices suffered because

of race, poverty, and sex have made some of us lose faith in the prom-
ises of democracy. But, with a focus on the individual human person
as the prime thing worth saving, we have made some starts in gen-
erating a renewed faith in the ideals of our democracy. There is hope
in the realization that some efforts to reestablish old ideals are suc-
ceeding: in the knowledge that an aroused public opinion can make
itself heard in the highest councils of the land; in the awareness that
individuals can band together to effect social and political change;
in the recognition that the law can be brought to serve decency. This
realization shapes the intellectual challenge of the end of the twentieth
century. Can the university in the years ahead serve the human needs
of all our people in their search for human dignity? Can it maintain
our belief in the power of scholarship to improve our understanding
of our neighbors and ourselves? Can it restore our confidence that
the unbiased and competent study of society by trained and dedicated
men and women can fashion for us the tools that can assist us in improving society? Can it provide a means for some students and some
members of the faculty to gain experience at the university with research on outstanding social problems, with a view not only to gaining
greater insight but also to proposing possible solutions based on careful research and critical discussion? If our society is to address itself
to some of our outstanding national needs — to imbue our political
practice with the expectation of strict ethical standards; to effect a
drastic reordering of our patterns of production; to redesign our
modes of consumption and our life style to be responsive to the requirements of our environment and the limitations in our resources;
to rehabilitate our core cities and our ghettos — then there are opportunities for the university to specialize in research that will exploit the
interest and vigor of many of our faculty and students, and give the
students the kind of background and expertise that can lead to exciting and rewarding careers that contribute to social progress.

Clearly, if we undertake to produce graduates who understand what our democracy is about, if we expect them to put public service and the welfare of the people before their own self-interest, we must insure that the universities see themselves as places where thoughtful and incisive learning and debate provide reasoned understanding of the problems of human beings and particularly of the problems inherent in this most difficult of all forms of government, the American democracy. We must expect that the college years will give our students some awareness of the dimensions of the problems.

A national committee of social and behavioral scientists has already reported that

> There can be little doubt that the behavioral and social sciences will become better basic sciences if their methods and findings are repeatedly and continuously tested for relevance to actual social behavior. An academically sound and organizationally firm base is needed for the development of behavioral and social science that is applicable to the large problems of society. The attack on such problems should not wait for crises to call attention to social pathology but should be on a continuing and long-range basis, with full attention given also to the rich theoretical contributions that can be made. Through research on genuine social problems, social scientists can improve the substance of their fields according to their own aspirations, while also serving society.[7]

Thus an increasingly strong interplay between the ivory tower and the marketplace may be needed for the welfare of the social sciences themselves and for other parts of the university including especially the professional schools. Because of the increasing focus on the professions that has characterized the interest of students during the past few years, universities have a special responsibility to insure that each professional school they sponsor undertakes rigorously to transmit the intellectual disciplines upon which the profession

---

[7] Behavioral and Social Sciences Survey Committee, *The Behavioral and Social Sciences: Outlook and Needs* (Englewood Cliffs, N.J.: Prentice-Hall, 1969).

rests, and that each has a program to seek the basic understanding without which the profession will not prosper. The experience of a university in engaging in the search for truth should fructify all the school's activities: provide basic understanding for the lawyers to insure that the law will serve the freedom of men; for doctors to help medicine add to the total meaning of men's lives; for social workers to understand that knowledge and research are needed as well as caring about our neighbors if we are to break through the awful cycle of poverty that imprisons so many of our citizens.

The demands of our society challenge us to lend the vitality of the ivory tower to the solution of the much more difficult problems of the marketplace, where a jump must be made from the security of knowledge to the insecurity of decision.

Regardless of the rigor of the intellectual requirements being placed upon our universities by the problems of society, there is an even more difficult demand arising out of the emerging belief that only through equal access to higher education for all our citizens can we hope to redress the inequities that exist in our society. The decision to move toward equal access introduces problems of a different order from those to which most of us are accustomed. In the commitment to equal access lies the decisive component of the transition to the third period in the history of America's universities.

With the coming of the second half of the twentieth century, the marketplace looks to the university with a new expectation: that the university will provide social mobility and increasing opportunity for participation in the fruits of an affluent society for those whom society has disadvantaged over the years — for members of minority ethnic groups, for young people who come from deprived socioeconomic backgrounds, and, in a somewhat different way, for women. Society still believes that higher education reduces the effects of social stratification and increases an individual's earning power, and these benefits are sought by the new groups that are emerging as the clients of higher education.

The problems of ethnic minorities and of women have been much discussed, but it may be worth quoting Lord Eric Ashby on the effects of social class upon access to higher education:

> A . . . fact which impresses itself upon the observer from Britain is one which an American observer would notice also in Britain, namely that neither country has succeeded in eliminating the effects of social class upon access to higher education. Both countries have made great efforts to do so, in different ways. In Britain it can be said with confidence that no one who is offered a place in a university need turn it down through lack of money; the limiting factor is lack of places. Subject to a reasonable means test of parents' income, a sum sufficient for fees and maintenance is paid from public funds to every student enrolled in a university or college of education or college in the public sector. Notwithstanding this, children whose parents are in lower income groups (or who come from low socioeconomic background) are seriously underrepresented in British universities. In America it can be said with equal confidence that a much higher proportion of the age group can find a place in a college, but, as in Britain, the children whose parents come from a low socioeconomic background are underrepresented. . . . [O]ne of the reports of the Carnegie Commission shows an ominous positive correlation between income group of parents and enrollment of their children, not only in universities and four-year colleges but even in two-year community colleges. Both in America and Britain this underrepresentation is not attributable to lack of money alone. . . . [S]ome of the poor do not want to go to college.[8]

It is true that many poor students do find their way to college. Particularly at my own institution, the City University of New York, which has been tuition-free from the time of its founding over a hundred and twenty-five years ago, the number of students from low socioeconomic groups is impressive; but in higher education gen-

---

[8] Ashby, *Any Person, Any Study*, pp. 19–20.

erally, the odds favor young people from the middle and upper income groups. As we turn our attention to providing an opportunity for many of those who have been excluded from higher education to continue to develop educationally beyond the high school, we find that the focus of our undertaking must shift to embrace a larger horizon than the one I have been discussing. One device that is being tried in an attempt to attack this problem is as old as the land-grant colleges — open admissions. This procedure casts doubt on the efficiency and fairness of the tests that have been widely used to determine whether or not a student should be admitted as a participant in higher education. Everyone knows that these tests are subject to a wide margin of error in individual cases, but the prospect of ignoring them in the admissions process causes shudders to pass through many a faculty body and raises the awful specter of a lowering of academic standards. We must recognize, however, that our diverse and adaptable educational system has always accommodated graduates of our high schools from even the lowest quartile of achievement, provided they could pay the tuition asked by whatever college was willing to have them. The present proposal is to admit many more students of lowest academic achievement. Admitting these students to some of our existing institutions has raised many new questions: Are our present universities providing the kinds of education these "new" students want to receive? *Should* the children of the poor and members of ethnic minorities attend the kind of college that "transmits intellectual disciplines and seeks the truth"?

Is a liberal education the kind of significant preparation for personal fulfillment and ethical social responsibility that we have claimed all these years? Are our routine references to "maintenance of standards" appropriate or are they clichés that we should reexamine in the light of students' needs?

Will open admissions to existing institutions increase the percentage of children from lower socioeconomic groups who attend?

Can substantial progress be made in increasing the success rate of the
"new" students? Can provision be made for accommodating students
from all age groups? From all walks of life? From all interest groups?
Should the universities undertake these tasks or are new institutions
needed?

Obviously I shall not try to address myself to all these questions
and the many others that must be asked. But I should think that one
of the first jobs of a new administration would be to sort out those
questions that should be considered by people now on campus, and
those that others should be encouraged to tackle. All members of a
university community will want to participate in deciding whether
the problem of universal access is one to whose solution they wish to
devote their resources. If the answer is "Yes," the faculty and students will surely want to give their thoughtful attention to discussion
and evaluation of the questions affecting the curriculum. The National Institute of Education should probably encourage an explora-
tion of the needs and potentials of new kinds of institutions. But the
procedures and problems associated with receiving the "new students" in existing institutions probably require large-scale investigation and experimentation such as that which is now in progress at
the City University of New York, where a policy of open admissions
became effective in the fall of 1970. The information now available
is inadequate to provide reliable results to serve as a basis of policy
decisions elsewhere, but a continuing longitudinal study is in progress,
and there are some results that may be worth reporting.

Under our program, all graduates of New York City high schools
were guaranteed places in the university, irrespective of the quality of
their high school work. I should stop to point out that the City University includes not only several well-known liberal arts colleges like
the City College of New York and Hunter College, but also a large
number of community colleges. When open admissions became a
practice not all competitive principles in admissions were eliminated.

Students who had graduated from high school with B averages or who had graduated in the top half of their high school class were guaranteed places in the senior colleges, while all others were allocated among the two-year community colleges. In earlier years the four-year colleges had had a requirement of a B average based on selected academic subjects, and in several of these colleges a higher requirement had been in force.

The City University experiment differs from prior practices of open admissions primarily in the decision to try to avoid the high attrition rates that have often characterized open admissions by providing programs of remediation and other support services that have never before been attempted on such a massive scale, and by determining that academic standards must be maintained in the university. The assumption is made that our established institutions, providing, as they do, a diverse mixture of "disciplines and recipes, challenges which stretch the mind and codified techniques which merely stuff it," will accommodate the diversity of students who will come to the campuses.[9] This assumption can well be challenged.

Let me give some preliminary results of the ongoing longitudinal study that contribute to the understanding of certain of the questions which I formulated earlier.

Has open admissions increased the percentage of students from low socioeconomic groups? The data available are not adequate for a complete answer to the question, but they are impressive nonetheless. A questionnaire addressed to the entering freshmen in the fall of 1971 finds that 10 percent were from families with incomes under $3,700, and an additional 10 percent were from families under $5,000. Almost 70 percent of the freshmen reported family incomes of less than $12,000. These results are based on responses from 7,500 freshmen; the total class included about 34,000 students.[10]

---

9 See Ashby, *Any Person, Any Study*, p. 31.

10 David E. Lavin in an unpublished report, 1973.

The Open Admissions Program did succeed in establishing a racial mix in the university's freshman class that closely approximated the racial proportions found in the city's high school graduating class.[11]

Twelve percent of the entering class considered that it needed remedial help in English, and 22 percent in mathematics. Preparing for a better job was considered a very important reason for attending college by 67 percent of the respondents, and fairly important by an additional 26 percent; but getting a broad general education and learning to help others were objectives of fair or great importance also to over 80 percent of the respondents.[12] Most interesting, perhaps, is the evidence that the "new" students (those who would not have qualified under earlier requirements), who constituted nearly 40 percent of the freshman class in the senior colleges in 1970 and nearly two thirds of the freshman class in the community colleges, were more successful in completing college work than the national average of all students, as reflected in the March 1971 *Report on Higher Education*.[13] This report estimates, on the basis of an analysis of a number of earlier reports dealing with various phases of the subject, that fewer than half of the more than one million young people who enter college in the United States each year will complete two years of study, and only about one third will ever complete a four-year course of study. In contrast, about 55 percent of the City University's "new" students completed two years of work,[14] and there is evidence that substantially

---

[11] See David E. Lavin and Barbara Jacobson, "Open Admissions at the City University of New York: A Description of Academic Outcomes after Three Semesters" (City University of New York, April 1973).

[12] See note 10, above.

[13] *Report on Higher Education* (Washington, D.C.: U.S. Government Printing Office, 1971), p. 12.

[14] Office of Program and Policy Research, City University of New York, "Open Admissions at the City University of New York: A Description of Academic Outcomes after Two Years" (June 1974), tables 3.9, 3.10, 3.11, 3.12.

more than one third of the new students who entered the senior colleges will ultimately earn a bachelor's degree.[15]

The attainment of a bachelor's degree is, however, only one of the problems. The new students, in common with many of the middle-class students who have been the clients of higher education for many years, see education explicitly as a means for social advancement and for better opportunity in a very difficult job market. But anecdotal information from a wide variety of faculty who are teaching the "open admissions" students tends to confirm that they want what they view as the "real thing," a high quality education that can provide the basis for the careers they seek. Many of those who succeed want to go on to professional careers or to careers in scholarship. Nevertheless, with this new student population, with new backgrounds and goals, many of the problems are magnified that confronted the universities when they moved into their second period of development, from their ivory tower orientation to the broader scope provided by the elective system. The new students constitute a challenge to the faculty for, as one of our distinguished visiting professors reported, they are very attractive and very eager, but they are not well educated. These new students do, indeed, come from a background that has not sent many of its sons and daughters to college. But that is one of the truly exciting features of being part of an institution like the City University. The new students also provide a challenge to teaching even more demanding than that posed during the storm of student revolt that swept so many of our campuses not too long ago. In the remedial programs, the imagination, dedication, and sheer stamina that are required may be enough to discourage many a teacher. But the challenge is also welcomed and enjoyed by many, and success is probably sweeter for those who succeed in the remedia-

---

[15] "Student Retention and Graduation at the City University of New York, September 1970 Enrollees through Eight Semesters" (Office of the Chancellor, April 1975).

tion program than elsewhere in collegiate teaching. Unfortunately, the experiments in remediation have been so various at the several colleges of our system that there are no statistical results reliable enough to report.

The whole subject of remediation does, however, raise questions about the role of the university in America, whether or not it participates in the ongoing experiment with universal access. At the City University, we embarked on the difficult and expensive remediation program because we were determined to give the new students we were welcoming to our campuses a fair chance to succeed. But many of them have come to the postsecondary experience unequipped with the most basic tools of a literate citizen.

Many of the students in our high schools are receiving a superb education; many are hopelessly undereducated. Why have we not made greater progress in understanding the nature of the problems being faced by the school systems in our large northern cities and in many parts of the South, and in preparing our teachers to handle them? Have the universities been seeking the truth in this difficult field with the diligence and intelligence that we should expect of them? Whatever the situation in the past, this is an area which in the decades ahead should have the very best attention that the universities, in cooperation with the citizenry and officials of our cities, can provide.

Although the City University's experiment is based on the assumption that the new students want to and should attend established institutions, all the students do have the opportunity to pursue vocational programs in the community colleges. The rapid growth of community colleges in the United States provides a viable alternative to the established four-year colleges for many new students. But there is a trend, nationwide, for these colleges to undervalue those of their programs that are specially geared to their communities' needs. The years ahead will surely require a reexamination of the meaning of undergraduate education and of the types of postsecondary experiences that will best provide opportunities for growth for individual students. There are already proprietary institutions, open universities, educational activities run by industries and by the military. There are already students, particularly women, who return for a formal education when they are mature. There are already many faculty members who move back and forth between the university on one hand and government or industry on the other. There are already many students who take time before completing work for a degree to gain experience away from the campus, and who return when their motivation is clarified and their purposes firm. All these perturbations on the standard pattern of four years of college, following immediately after secondary school, will be magnified in the years ahead, and each university will want to determine what role it will play in supporting and facilitating the education of men and women in ways and at times that will most enrich their lives. This is a time of educational ferment. No university will want to miss the opportunity to play a vital role.

It is important, if our total system of higher education is to meet its obligations, that each campus assess where its best contributions will lie in the light of its history, its resources, its commitments, and the community it serves. The growth of multicampus systems and of state coordinating boards for higher education poses a threat to the autonomy that a university must have as it undertakes an assessment of the part it should play. But it is important that the task of enlarging educational opportunity for those who seek postsecondary education be undertaken by a significant number of institutions throughout the land.

Whatever the response an institution makes to this most recent call from the marketplace, it must remember Lord Eric Ashby's warning that we must preserve

> a thin clear stream of excellence to provide new ideas, new techniques, and the statesmanlike treatment of complex social and

political problems. Without the renewal of this excellence, a nation can drop to mediocrity in a generation. The renewal of excellence is expensive: the highly gifted student needs informal instruction, intimate contact with other first-class minds, opportunities to learn the discipline of dissent from men who have themselves changed patterns of thought; in a word . . . this sort of student needs to be treated as *elite*. . . . It is commonly assumed that America has to choose between one or other of two patterns of higher education: mass or elite. I would deny this assumption.[16]

This is the consuming issue in higher education today. Can we have excellence and equality or must we choose between them? There are many who believe that experiments with open admissions should be dropped before they ruin our institutions, and many others who are convinced that only in the direction of open admissions lies salvation. This severe testing of our educational system's resilience and power comes at a time when our universities face a problem new in the history of higher education in the United States. For the first time, the growth of the system is coming to an end. In a system that is no longer expanding, only the most rigorous determination, combined with truly remarkable insight, can preserve opportunities for innovation and change. It may well be that the multiversity that has served the country with distinction in the decades just past will prove to be the wrong concept for the end of the millennium. But multifunctional or simple, private or public, part of a multicampus system or leading a completely autonomous life, some version of the university will, I am convinced, continue to be called upon to be responsive to the human and social needs of the people in whatever ways intellectual achievements of high order and a determination to seek the truth can help. Somehow the university must preserve its power to create new knowledge, acquire wisdom, and provide a critical evaluation of society for the sake of society's self-renewal; it must provide

---

[16] Ashby, *Any Person, Any Study*, pp. 101–102.

appropriate stimulation and participation for truly gifted students; and it must protect its ivory tower if it would continue to play a constructive role in the marketplace. In these tasks lie the challenge and the despair of those who would participate in building the future of our universities.

David Pierpont Gardner

Forces for Change in American Higher Education

Universities and colleges in the United States are confronted with an array of fiscal, educational, social, and political problems as unrelenting as they are seemingly unresolvable within the context of established educational conventions.

The higher learning in America, for example, is expected to cope with the diverse wants and needs of a student body and faculty more heterogeneous and less patient with the settled form of learning than before; with shifting governmental and social priorities which tend both to spread and to diminish resources available to colleges and universities; with costs which are rising at a faster rate than that of the nation's production of goods and services as a whole; with the rise of public interest in higher education and the consequent intervention of various governmental agencies in the internal affairs of higher education institutions; and with the unmet educational needs of adults and unequal educational opportunities for the poor.

Thus, single-valued forecasts and perspectives which tended to dominate academic planning and expansion in the 1960's ought not to limit the present range of policy options nor compromise promising

© 1976 by The Third Century Corporation.

alternative educational strategies, for it seems quite likely that the uncritical expansion of our institutions of higher education along established and familiar lines is, for the most part, a thing of the past. "Hardly anywhere," as Roy Niblett has observed, "is it generally believed that the recipe for meeting the next twenty years is to continue to do, only better, what has been done in the last twenty." [1] The more likely prospect is that higher education in this decade and the next can be expected to assimilate or at least accommodate a variety of alternative, experimental, and unconventional educational forms and structures. Five major forces for change will give rise to these innovations:

1. *The impact on the educational system by the drive for greater access to higher education and more equal educational opportunity.* Enrollments in America's colleges and universities have doubled every ten to fifteen years for the past century and they doubled again during the 1960's. Roughly 4 percent of college-age youth were enrolled in America's institutions of higher learning in 1900; today more than 40 percent are enrolled, and estimates are that nearly two out of three of the age group will be enrolled as this century closes. The pressure to expand has been and will remain relentless, although the rate of increase will drop and the pattern of formal enrollments will shift somewhat within the established learning system away from the senior colleges and universities and toward the community colleges and post-secondary vocational and technical schools and institutions. The nation is moving from mass- to universal-access higher education, or perhaps more accurately, to universal postsecondary education.

The most evident and consistent pressure for expansion in recent years has come from the poor, the educationally disadvantaged, and the ethnic minorities, primarily Blacks, Chicanos, and Native Americans, for whom higher education has not been a real option until

---

[1] W. R. Niblett, "Issues and Choices," in W. R. Niblett and R. F. Butts, eds., *Universities Facing the Future* (San Francisco: Jossey-Bass, 1972), p. 3.

now, and from the federal government, politically attuned to the demands and generally supportive of such educational aspirations and stirrings. The proportion of such college-age youth enrolling in America's colleges and universities has steadily risen in recent years owing to the maturing of the comprehensive secondary school system, the growth and development of the community college system with its "open door" policy of admissions, and the huge student aid program which has so dramatically increased since the close of World War II, both in scope of program and in scale of assistance.

As Cerych and Furth have suggested, the demand for higher education, especially in recent years, "has led not only to massive expansion of enrollments but also to a change in the clientele of higher education, i.e., to a considerably increased variety and greater heterogeneity of aptitudes, abilities, motivations and expectations of students with regard to their future education, professional careers and life in general." [2]

As recently as a decade ago, it was assumed that the extension of educational opportunities to the poor, the educationally disadvantaged, and the ethnic minorities could be accomplished merely by availing such new students of the same programs, resources, and academic conventions as had been extended in earlier years to the upwardly mobile middle class. The assumption proved to be false not only because a conflict ensued between the new students and the forms and practices of established institutions but also because of the unanticipated rejection of conventional academic values by significant numbers of middle-class students, what Martin Trow calls the "involuntary student" and what Lord Ashby describes as the "semi-drafted student" — students, in short, who feel compelled to attend college for educationally irrelevant reasons.

---

[2] L. Cerych and D. Furth, "On the Threshold of Mass Higher Education," in Niblett and Butts, eds., *Universities Facing the Future*, p. 19.

Thus, America's universities and colleges found themselves fighting on two fronts in the 1960's, and they are still skirmishing today. The turmoil carries very real implications for the life pattern of the educational system itself and long-accepted values of academic life: "patient inquiry, the sequential development of ideas, the emphasis on reasoned discussion and criticism, the continual reference to evidence, and the special attention to negative evidence," as Martin Trow describes it.[3]

The academic environment can no longer be regarded as the "sole preserve" of the faculty and administration, Clark Kerr has observed, for students will take a more active interest than in the past in the quality of teaching, the form and substance of the curriculum, the supporting counseling and advisory services, and the costs to them of pursuing their studies.[4]

2. *An inability to fund higher education in the future as in the past.* Higher education is facing more than the financial crisis about which much has already been written. It is faced as well with the gloomy prospect that if the system merely grows and spends money consistent with established forms and patterns, it will almost certainly soon fall well short of what is needed merely to survive. The Carnegie Commission has reported that expenditures by the nation's colleges and universities approximated 1 percent of the GNP in 1960, 2 percent in 1970 and, if present trends persist, would equal roughly 3.3 percent in 1980, even though not more than 2.7 percent is expected to be forthcoming from the various funding agencies or parties by that time. Budgets will be harder to come by; enrollments will be relatively stable (at least in conventional academic institu-

---

[3] Martin Trow, "The Expansion and Transformation of Higher Education," *International Review of Education* 18, no. 1 (The Hague, 1972) : 71.

[4] Clark Kerr, "The Administration of Higher Education in an Era of Change and Conflict" (First David D. Henry Lecture, University of Illinois at Urbana-Champaign, 1972), pp. 21–22; published as "Administration in an Era of Change and Conflict," in *Educational Record* 54, no. 1 (Winter 1973) : 38–46.

tions) ; competition for resources by other social agencies and service institutions will become more intense; costs will rise more rapidly than the GNP owing to the labor-intensive nature of educational institutions generally and, as Clark Kerr has suggested, "the lack of productivity increase will become a widely discussed naked fact instead of a harsh reality hidden behind the cloak of expanding numbers." [5]

Colleges and universities have generally responded to these fiscal pressures not by reconsidering goals or by altering the educational process, but instead by across-the-board cost-cutting, and by delaying expenditures that would otherwise have been made on ordinary administrative support services and the development of academic programs. Such economies are only marginal and temporary, however, for these measures avoid coming to grips with the problem of productivity in the teaching and learning process itself.[6] This is not to say that such economies bear no relationship to the effective performance of an institution's educational mission and to its momentum. They do, but in less visible and immediate ways. Real increases in productivity will occur only if the educational process itself is changed — that is, only if the time and spread of curriculum, the form and methods of instruction, and the relationship of the student to the institution are somehow modified.

There is no doubting the fiscal crisis afflicting the higher learning in America. It is real, omnipresent and foreboding. The reasons are many and complex: inflation; competing social programs, especially in government-sponsored welfare and health services; a prolonged and costly war in Southeast Asia; student unrest in the 1960's and

---

[5] Ibid., p. 19.

[6] See Virginia Smith, "More for Less: A New Priority," in American Council on Education, *Universal Higher Education*, Logan Wilson and Olive Mills, eds. (Background papers for participants in the Fifty-fourth Annual Meeting of the American Council on Education, Washington, D.C., 1971), p. 127; published by the American Council on Education (Washington, D.C., 1972).

early 1970's; disenchantment with research; and a startling loss of public confidence in the entire enterprise.[7] "Taxpayers, legislators and private donors," as Lord Eric Ashby has reported, "want universities to demonstrate (i) that they can govern themselves in reasonable tranquility; (ii) that they are being run efficiently . . . ; and (iii) that they can restore a consensus about 'a unifying set of purposes — purposes that the supporting public can understand and defer to.' "[8]

Pressures arising out of these problems have translated into institutional budgets inadequate to maintain, much less to strengthen, existing programs and practices or to permit growth within the conventional context. It should be evident that any significant expansion of the system along familiar lines must anticipate some wearing away of standards and capability.

3. *A marked increase of interest and involvement in the internal affairs of higher education by government at all levels.* "The greatest change in governance now going on is not the rise of student power or faculty power but the rise of public power," Clark Kerr has noted.[9]

Public control of America's colleges and universities is steadily on the rise. The involvement of state budget experts, governors, legislative committees, federal agencies, and the courts in the internal affairs of our institutions of higher education is unquestionably increasing and in the most fundamental of ways. Formerly independent institutions of higher learning are now "coordinated" if not actually merged, as state government makes them subject to essentially the same bureaucratic controls, measures, expectations, and efficiencies as apply to any other "state agencies." Massive bureaucracies admin-

---

[7] See Earl F. Cheit, *The New Depression in Higher Education: A Study of Financial Conditions at 41 Colleges and Universities* (New York: McGraw-Hill, 1971).

[8] Eric Ashby, "The Great Reappraisal," in Niblett and Butts, eds., *Universities Facing the Future*, p. 36.

[9] Kerr, "Administration . . . in an Era of Change and Conflict," p. 21.

istering statewide systems are increasing everywhere both in number and in authority.

Regulations flowing from such state systems of higher education have tended to standardize course offerings for lower-division work, fix standard academic calendars, mandate uniform teaching loads, set common salary schedules for faculty, and establish standard formulae for space utilization and the acquisition of books for libraries — often as though there were no distinctions among institutions in the quality of their work, in their respective missions, in their learning environments, in the desires and abilities of their student bodies, in their basic character, in their inner selves.

It is equally true, of course, that the rise in public power and the corresponding diminution of institutional autonomy have produced conditions favorable to the creation of new or affiliated institutions with unconventional approaches to teaching and learning which, in earlier years and times, would not have been tolerated, much less encouraged, by the educational establishment — such new ventures, for example, as the Empire State College in New York, the Extended University in California, the State University of Nebraska, and Minnesota Metropolitan State College. As might be expected, the non-traditional programs fostered by these institutions are perceived by some as a boon both to higher education and to those it serves for they promise to break the time, space, and age constraints which have always bound conventional learning patterns. They are seen by others as debasing the essential nature of the university itself together with its standards and further dispersing scarce educational resources.

Whatever the view, the fact remains that a heightened public interest in the affairs of our colleges and universities tends, over time, to make them more alike and to enlarge the scope of their services, the breadth of their programs, and the number and nature of persons deserving of their talents, time, resources, and programs.

4. *The preference of some full-time students to mix part-time study with work and the growing desire of the fully employed to combine work on the job or at home with periodic full-time or part-time study.* Pressure on the higher learning system to expand and accommodate the educational needs of adult students wishing to study part-time and the desire of some full-time students of college age to opt for part-time study is a relatively new phenomenon but one quite likely, in the long run, to effect significant changes in the form and structure of American higher education.

Adults, because of work schedules, family or home responsibilities, financial constraints, and cultural or geographical isolation cannot now effectively enroll in most degree programs offered by America's colleges and universities; and this is especially true of the more prestigious universities. The impediments are both philosophical and procedural and are deeply rooted in institutional prejudice and practice. Adult students seeking further educational opportunity do so for a variety of reasons: to conclude degree programs started but unfinished in earlier years; to shift careers at midpoint; to improve competencies in established career patterns; to enhance intellectual, social, cultural, political, and environmental understanding and awareness; and to initiate studies in later life because the opportunity or motivation was lacking earlier.

A recent report of the Carnegie Commission on Higher Education, in a general discussion of the flow of students into and through the formal structure of higher education, suggests educationally and socially relevant reasons for encouraging the enrollment of adults:

> Society would gain if work and study were mixed throughout a lifetime, thus reducing the sense of sharply compartmentalized roles of isolated students v. workers and of youth v. isolated age. The sense of isolation would be reduced if more students were also workers and if more workers could also be students; if the ages mixed on the job and in the classroom in a more structured type of community; if all the members of the community valued both

study and work and had a better chance to understand the flow of life from youth to age. Society would be more integrated across the lines that now separate students and workers, youth and age.[10]

If American higher education should rid itself of barriers to adult part-time study it would also provide options for the "involuntary" student of college-age now attending full-time: either deferred enrollment, or recurring periods of study, or continuous part-time study mixed with work. In short, it would have cleared away the assumption, as Ashby puts it, "that full-time education should be digested all in one gulp, from age 5 to age 22." [11] It would also introduce highly motivated adults into the system and reduce the enrollments of "semi-drafted" students whose presence now tends to weaken the overall effectiveness of the learning process.

The changing nature of the job market itself may very well prove to be the most important single influence in bringing about the interweaving of work and study that the Carnegie Commission favors. The coordinating of work and study based on job structure may come to indicate the desirability of a pattern which reduces the period of time spent in early life for formal education, while increasing the periods of study available later in accordance with a schedule of alternating periods of study and work — or as some labor–management agreements in recent years have called for, a blending of part-time work with part-time study.

Gösta Rehn, director of manpower and social affairs for the Organization for Economic Cooperation and Development, anticipates that the established forms and patterns of the higher learning will be profoundly affected by already perceived trends in the more industrialized nations of the world, for example, a progressive reduction in the hours of work per week accompanied by a rising level of

---

[10] The Carnegie Commission on Higher Education, *Less Time, More Options: Education Beyond the High School* (New York: McGraw-Hill, 1971), pp. 1–2.

[11] Eric Ashby, *Any Person, Any Study: An Essay on Higher Education in the United States* (New York: McGraw-Hill, 1971), p. 99.

real income per hour, an expansion of the service sector of the economy with its more flexible working schedule, a rising rate of urbanization accompanied by changes in life styles and values which militate against rigid and intense working conditions and for a more varied and enriching pattern of life experiences.

5. *The influence of communication technology on the typical time, space, and age requirements of the conventional learning process — what the Carnegie Commission calls "the first great technological revolution in five centuries."* Of the revolutions taking place in our time, one of the most significant and exciting, from the viewpoint of educators, must surely be the one in telecommunications and educational technology. The impact of scientific and technological breakthroughs in this area will, in very major ways, affect the entire educational establishment, and perhaps higher education even more than the lower grades.

The new electronics has already impacted research and administrative methods in higher education and is now moving to transform the library and the teaching process itself. The instructional uses of such devices as cable television, cable and television technology in general, microwave, videophone, microfiche, digitalization and switching, long-range facsimile, communication satellites, and the computer, among others, may offer the greatest single opportunity for academic change on and off campus higher education has had in its history. It will be possible for education to be brought "to the sick, the handicapped, the aged, the prisoners, the members of the armed forces, persons in remote areas, and to many adults who could attend classes on campus but who will find instruction at home more convenient. It can create new uses for leisure time, can facilitate job to job movement through new training, and can improve community participation by imparting greater skill and knowledge to citizens." [12]

---

[12] The Carnegie Commission on Higher Education, *The Fourth Revolution: Instructional Technology in Higher Education* (New York: McGraw-Hill, 1972), pp. 1–2.

As the multi-channel, closed-circuit educational TV systems develop and cable television expands its network, satellites will tend to diminish the now-dominant position of the networks, or at least will very likely tend to force them to diversify. As the use of satellites increases, there will be an obvious trend toward the internationality of learning as the barriers of distance, geography, race, nationality, language, and religion are modified — a matter posing immense problems and suggesting immensely exciting possibilities, especially for educators.

Within the context of domestic educational change, these forms of technology will most surely be converted to uses implicating virtually every aspect of our educational institutions. They will influence our times and places of instruction and our methods of teaching and curricula. After a period of careful and systematic experimentation with such forms of education they may well prove to be desirable modes of instruction for large numbers of students while being more cost-effective as well.

Nevertheless, educational technology has not yet been fully and effectively employed by higher education for a variety of reasons. These include the insulation of technological resources from the educational process itself; the absence of cost data on the instructional use of such technology and standardized patterns of utilization; and a reluctance to expect or require faculty knowledge of and proficiency in the use of technology for educational purposes. System is the basic imperative of all technology.[13]

The effective and economical use of educational technology by colleges and universities can be anticipated only if new collaborative arrangements (intra- and inter-institutional) and a systems approach to the educational process are successfully pursued. The benefits that

---

[13] See Bernard Trotter, *Television and Technology in University Teaching: A Report to the Committee on University Affairs, and the Committee of Presidents of Universities of Ontario* (Toronto: Council of Ontario Universities, 1970), p. 50.

such technologies can provide, of course, are substantial. They include the duplication of high-quality instruction at low cost for convenient and repeated access by students in residence and off campus; individualization of instruction; collaborative arrangements among institutions having common academic interests, irrespective of geographical considerations; improved opportunities for independent study and a richer mix of course work and methods of instruction for students; fewer routine teaching duties for faculty members, especially at the more elementary levels; and opportunities for research and increased understanding of basic learning processes.[14]

The Carnegie Commission has predicted that by the year 2000, "a significant portion of instruction in higher education on campus may be carried on through informational technology — perhaps in a range of 10 to 20 percent. It certainly will penetrate much further than this into off-campus instruction at levels beyond the secondary school — in fact, it may become dominant there at a level of 80 percent or more."[15] Should the Commission's prediction be realized, future generations of students will surely be less campus-bound than have been those of the past, while at the same time the campus will become an even more central link between the present condition of society and the future. By the turn of the century, technology in various forms may well have transformed the campus from a center of learning into a learning center — one which houses a highly mobile population of students and scholars, a small resident population for study primarily at the most advanced levels, a panoply of laboratories for residential research, and an integrated network of libraries, computers, television, and other teaching resources designed as much for residential as for off-campus study and research; in short, a network

---

[14] For an elaboration of these benefits and a thorough detailing of the educational implications of the new technology, see the Carnegie Commission's *The Fourth Revolution*, especially pp. 4–7.

[15] Ibid., p. 1.

of associations, arrangements, and resources that will permit the student to have the university or college with him at home, at work, and at his leisure throughout his lifetime.

The educational response to these and related pressures by institutions of higher learning in the United States has been as unsure as it has been uneven. In general, such educational initiatives as there have been are either new and often student-initiated (and sometimes student-designed) academic programs developed and offered mostly within conventional settings, or what have come to be called non-traditional studies, largely intended to offer new student constituencies newly designed or already established academic programs in novel ways and at times and places convenient to the learners.

The development of student-initiated programs has resulted primarily from the generational revolt of the 1960's and from the demand for curricular options matching the heterogeneity of the American student body. Self-designed programs range all the way from the small and informal, involving a very few students, to those available to an entire student body.[16] While it is generally assumed that students will consult with faculty members in planning their academic programs, they are ordinarily expected to arrange interdisciplinary courses of study responsive to their special learning interests and individual styles by drawing on any combination of courses, tutorials, and independent study options available within the host university or college.

As part of the trend, learning contracts entered into between a university or college and a student — sometimes formally written — have been gaining favor in recent years. Evergreen State College, in the state of Washington, has drawn considerable interest and much applause for its program of "contracted studies." The pertinent

---

16 See Paul R. Givens, "Student-Designed Curricula," *Research Currents* (Washington, D.C.: ERIC Clearinghouse on Higher Education, 1972), p. 3.

reference in the college's *Bulletin* reads: "For a substantial part of your career at Evergreen, you may work in contracted studies. Using this pattern, you as an individual or as a member of a small group sharing your interests can sign up with a faculty member or other staff member to earn credit by doing a specific project, carrying out a specific investigation, mastering a specific skill, or dealing with a specific body of subject matter . . . . We call this arrangement a 'contract' for learning to emphasize that it is an agreement to do a piece of work and that it implies direct, mutual responsibility between you and the experienced person whom you have asked to help you."

Variations on the same theme are to be found in the curricular options of an increasing number of institutions, among them New College at the University of Alabama, New College in Florida, Simpson College in Iowa, Whittier College in California, and Ottawa College in Kansas.[17]

The nontraditional programs and alternative educational strategies currently in operation or under development can be fairly well typified within the framework suggested by the Educational Testing Service. This includes programs that extend existing curricula through new means to new students; programs that offer not only conventional education in unconventional ways to new students, but also new curricula, learning experiences, and degrees to both new and traditional student bodies; programs that seek to compress or accelerate the postsecondary learning experience, whether new or conventional, by such means as advanced placement, achievement tests, competency exams, year-round operations, and more compact curricula; and programs that are designed to certify competence but offer no instruction.

Scores of nontraditional programs have been undertaken by colleges and universities singly or through consortia in recent years. They

---

[17] For a more complete list of learning contract colleges and universities and student-designed programs, see Givens, "Student-Designed Curricula," pp. 5–6.

include New York's Empire State College, Minnesota Metropolitan State College, Union for Experimenting Colleges and Universities, The State University of Nebraska, California's Extended University, Lincoln State University in Illinois, and Florida International University's External Degree Program. Others are in the planning and early developmental stages, such as the Central New York Consortium for nontraditional secondary and higher education, the University of Hawaii's off-campus degree plans, the University of Maine's Bachelor of Liberal Studies for Adults, and the Wisconsin study now under way based upon the European principle of "education permanente." [18] The trial use in several American colleges and universities of some of the British Open University materials also bears review and monitoring as the evaluation of these experiments is prepared and reported.

The common purpose shared by these nontraditional programs is that they are intended to be less bound by conventional concepts of time, space, and age than now typifies the established learning process. Universities and colleges in the United States have ordinarily limited instruction in degree programs to a prearranged, scheduled sequence of courses for those of college age studying full time in residence on campus. It is true, of course, that the community colleges and urban universities and colleges have been more accommodating of part-time, commuting, and working students than have the major public and private universities and prestigious liberal arts colleges, whether in urban or rural settings. Nevertheless, the academic values implicit in the prevailing conventions have tended to discourage experimentation with fundamentally new educational concepts in much of the higher learning.

---

[18] For a comprehensive inventory and summary description of recent developments in nontraditional study, see John R. Valley, *Increasing the Options: Recent Developments in College and University Degree Programs* (Princeton: Educational Testing Service, 1972).

Most nontraditional programs as are in place or anticipated in the United States take relatively little account of their possible impact on the established learning system. Interaction between the nontraditional and the conventional is, seemingly, more inadvertent than intended. Thus, new colleges, schools, divisions, institutions, structures, and administrative procedures and processes are everywhere emerging, mostly as autonomous and self-generating units. Each is striving to establish itself before organized resistance to its unconventional academic program can assume form and direction. The most likely impediments will be introduced by the dominant institutions of higher learning, usually out of fear for a further scattering of scarce educational resources, and by government, mostly out of the desire to couple such politically attractive programs with the less academic, more vocationally-oriented and paraprofessional ones that comprise so much of the response to the new demand for postsecondary education. Either move, if successful, would blunt whatever momentum had been achieved at the time and, in the end, probably compromise nontraditional *academic* programs, whatever its positive effects in other parts of the postsecondary educational system.

There is, of course, much to be said for mounting such bold new initiatives within the nurturing environment of an entirely new institution whose present and future welfare depends upon the successful achievement of nontraditional educational objectives. Those responsible in such a setting can, among other things, settle upon their own administrative and admission procedures rather than confronting the task of revising those already in force. They can devise and design new curricula unencumbered by the constraints of others already in place, recruit and appoint a faculty committed to the purposes to which the new college or school is dedicated, and pursue resources and support with little regard to who may be hurt by a shift in the pattern of funding for higher education. In short, the range of discretion is

greater and the constraints are fewer, however demanding and difficult may be the task of giving life to a new institution.

New institutions generally, of course, are as vulnerable as they are
administratively attractive to persons determined to achieve major
gains within a short span of time. They can be blocked by more powerful interests without doing damage to or implicating an established
enterprise; they can be captured by competing interests for different
but related purposes; they can be embraced by influential interests
whose purpose is not to nurture but to smother; they can become too
closely associated with the fortunes of one charismatic personality
whose ill-timed departure would compromise the effort; and, in the
instance of educational institutions, they can be badly hurt by a hostile
or indifferent higher education community should it collectively
choose to boycott the entire effort by refusing to acknowledge the
essential worth and academic integrity of nontraditional study and
the transferability of credit earned in such programs.

Whether or not nontraditional programs in this country will have
a significant impact on American higher education is really quite uncertain. Each is encumbered by the negative influence of conventional
academic biases, by inadequate funding, or by hostile administrative
interests, unfavorable structural arrangements, disjunction between
its goals and those of its potential clients, or by all or some combination of these and similar impediments.

The educational quality of nontraditional study programs is also
an issue of major concern to academics who are supportive of these
unconventional educational initiatives as well as to traditional academics. The several regional accrediting associations are only now
beginning to grapple with the issue, as are other state and national
study commissions interested in the movement. Samuel Gould, for example, chairman of the prestigious Commission on Non-Traditional
Study, whose final report was submitted in 1973, has identified some
of the dangers: "(1) There is the danger of deterioration of stan-

dards; (2) there is the danger of the external degree being used too much as a political instrument and too little as an educational instrument; (3) there is the danger of curriculum content vagueness; (4) there is the danger that in the excitement of developing new ways of delivering instruction and credentialling people, the important and needed debate over what constitutes an educated person will continue to be postponed." [19]

The competence and motivation of the students; the adequacy of funding; the sufficiency of supporting library, laboratory, and counseling services; the knowledge, skill, and dedication of the faculty; the rigor of the program — these and related considerations bear upon the essential worth and integrity of any coherent academic program *leading to a degree*. Nontraditional study programs should be scrutinized no less in this regard than are established offerings (but surely not with greater zeal or bias than would normally attend a review of new programs proposed along familiar lines).[20]

Research and evaluation associated with the development of nontraditional and student-initiated programs, if carefully planned, amply funded, and meaningfully articulated with program development, can measurably contribute to the academic quality of new programs. It can also broaden our overall understanding of the learning process, the nature of maturation and motivation, and the adequacy of existing forms and processes of the established learning system. It is far from clear that such research and evaluation has been undertaken as innovative programs have developed in recent years. Most nontraditional programs have emerged during times of fiscal stringency. Under such circumstances, the allocation of scarce resources

---

[19] In John Valentine, "The Bold Vision and the Hard Road," *College Board Review*, no. 85 (Fall 1972) : 8.

[20] For a brief summary of how some nontraditional programs are coping with the quality issue, see Carol H. Shulman, "A Look at External Degrees," *College and University Bulletin* 25, no. 3 (November 1972) : 4–6.

to research and evaluation at the expense of program funding is too often seen as shortsighted and extravagant. Thus, few of the new programs have been purposely structured to include systematic corrective mechanisms which would assure a thorough evaluation and provide evidence of desired academic quality.

These difficulties notwithstanding, much can still be learned from systematic studies of potential student populations. Market research could well be aimed at revealing, among other things, the current level of felt need for university- or college-level degree programs among the adult population; the perceived functions of such education (certification, vocational training, retraining, or upgrading, general cultural interests, etc.); the perceived barriers to full-time study at the university or college level among the adult population; the perceived barriers to such part-time opportunities as presently exist; the educational needs within specific occupational groups; and the extent to which students enrolled in full-time programs of study would opt for part-time alternatives, were the latter available.

In the absence of extensive sampling and verifiable evidence, one can only suspect that the two major sources of positive attraction to nontraditional degree programs will prove to be a desire for greater time and space flexibility in gaining access to higher education, arising out of objective familial and financial impediments to easy full-time residential enrollment, and a negative view of established forms and modes of higher education, whether this negative valence be due to personal experience or to a contrary ideological view of traditional higher education. In order to respond to both of these needs, American higher education will find it necessary, on the one hand, to create flexible time–space arrangements and thereby facilitate access without basically changing the internal structure of curricula or the basic values which underlie them and, on the other hand, to create new programs and new modes of learning more responsive to the values and educational ideologies of individual students, which may or may not be so located in space and time as to make them more accessible than are existing traditional academic programs. No single response or model is likely to serve each group equally well.[21]

Controversy can be expected to surround the development and evolution of nontraditional programs as criticism continues to be heard concerning the concept and emergence of mass higher education in Europe and universal postsecondary education in America. Lord Eric Ashby's insightful observations in regard to this phenomenon are pertinent and deserving of an alert and attentive concern:

> [M]ass higher education, like mass production, is a different thing from "handmade" education or production. A lot of it is impersonal, even using techniques of videotape, TV, and correspondence courses. The experience of the London external degree and the promise of the Open University show that this can be done successfully. But there are still two kinds of education which demand a personal teacher-student relationship, for which there is no substitute. One is vocational, the education of master craftsmen and artists. To become an engraver on glass, or a silversmith, or a solo violinist, there is only one recipe: to be apprenticed to a master and to submit to his regime of discipline. The other is nonvocational, the education of the innovators in intellectual life and the pacesetters in cultural and moral standards. For this, too, there is only one recipe: the sustained dialectic with a master whose own intellectual and cultural achievements are distinguished. So, within the system of mass higher education, there must be opportunities for the intellect to be stretched to its capacity (the critical faculty sharpened to the point where it can change ideas), by close contact with men who are intellectual masters. Not many students are fit for this austere discipline or are willing to submit to it but those who are must be able to find it, or the thin clear stream of excellence on which society depends for innovation and for statesmanship will dry up. Personally I am not in favour of herding such talented students into special institutions. Talent and mediocrity can share the same central heating

---

[21] See Joseph Zelan and David P. Gardner, "Alternatives in Higher Education — Who Wants What?" in *Higher Education* 4 (1975): 317–33.

plant and cafeteria, and they should, for talent has to learn to operate in a world of mediocrity.[22]

There are many factors, of course, which will influence the direction of both traditional and unconventional forms of postsecondary education in the United States. The more crucial of them have been thoroughly discussed in reports issued by the Carnegie Commission: the learning environment, including both its facilitating and impeding characteristics and opportunities; the relative competitive attractiveness of education as against other options available for the use of the student's time; the student's inclination toward and adeptness at learning; monetary and nonmonetary reinforcement and rewards associated with learning; the effectiveness and accessibility of educational and learning programs and institutions; and methods of financing postsecondary education.[23]

"The movement toward recurrent lifetime education with adequate provision to offset personal income loss," the Commission has suggested, "appears to be a logical step for the last quarter of the Twentieth Century. Particularly in the United States where universal access to collegiate education is now nearly assured to all youth, the next step in the evolution of our educational system would seem to be the assurance that lifetime educational opportunities be within the reach of all motivated adults."

Whatever the outcome of present efforts to innovate and breathe change into the nation's institutions of higher learning, the very questioning by so many of the assumptions about *who* will partake of their programs, and *how*, *when*, and *where* they will do so, assures continuing efforts to deal unconventionally with the established forms and patterns of higher education in America.

----

22 Eric Ashby, *Adapting Universities to a Technological Society* (San Francisco: Jossey-Bass, 1974), pp. 142–43.

23 See especially *Toward a Learning Society: Alternative Channels to Life, Work, and Service* (New York: McGraw-Hill, 1973).

On the Meaning of the University
was set in Intertype Baskerville
with handset Baskerville Foundry display type,
printed by the University of Utah Printing Service,
and bound by Mountain States Bindery.
University of Utah presidential medallion
sculpted by Michael J. Nelson.
Typography by Donald M. Henriksen.
Design by Bailey-Montague & Associates.